Simple Hospitality

AN INVITATION TO ADD KINDNESS
TO YOUR EVERYDAY LIFE

Title: Simple Hospitality
Subtitle: An Invitation to Add Kindness to Your Everyday Life
Author: Jennifer Boyd
With Writer: Emily Osbourne
Graphic Design by: Mary Grace Burkett

JenniferBoydAuthor.com

Printed in the United States of America

With love to my parents, Beverly and Vernon Moline.
You are the ones who first modeled hospitality and
kindness, and I am blessed to be your daughter.

Table of Contents

Introduction 9

1 THE MINDSET OF SIMPLE HOSPITALITY 10

Keep Your Table Set 12

Gifts to Go 16

Encouragement with a Card 18

Bring the Fragrance of Flowers 22

Offer What You Have 26

2 GIVE THE GIFT OF KINDNESS 30

Make Your Home the Headquarters of Kindness 32

Traveling Kindness 36

Creative Kindness 40

Listen with Intention 44

Kindness and Gratitude 48

3 THE WRITTEN WORD 52

Send a Gift Through Special Words 54

Create a Lovely System 56

An Unexpected Note 60

Add a Special Surprise 64

Letters to Authors 66

4 TAKE HOSPITALITY ON THE ROAD 70

Tea Party to Go 72

Bring Dinner During Life Transitions 76

Send an Article 80

Overcome Obstacles to Make Something Special 84

Speak to the Manager 88

5 FRIENDSHIP AND OPENNESS 92

Openness Invites Joy 94

Make Time for Something New 98

Take a Chance and Give the Invitation 98

Look for Someone Who Needs a Friend 104

Tell Me Your Story 106

6 PARTIES AND GATHERINGS 110

Get in The Party Mindset 112

Creative Ways to Celebrate 116

Gather People to Help in a Difficult Time 120

Invite Your Child's Teacher to Dinner 122

Anniversaries 126

7 MAKING INTENTIONAL MEMORIES 130

The Standout Days 132

Turn a Negative Memory into a Fun Celebration 136

Celebrate the Beginning and the Ending 138

The Banana Bread Day 142

Intentional Sporty Memories 144

8 CREATIVE PARTIES 148

Make Friendly Connections 150

Host a Gratitude Party 152

Know and Be Known 156

Think About It 160

Receive with Gratitude 162

9 TRADITIONS AND MEMORIES 166

Beauty Through a Weekly Tradition 168

Beauty in a Holiday Tradition 170

Share the Stories of Your Holiday Traditions 172

The Beauty of a New Tradition 176

Record and Rewrite to Make Anything Special 178

10 THE PLEASURE OF WRITING 182

Menu and Name Tags for your Table 184

From My Kitchen to Yours 188

Write Important Advice to Share with Loved Ones 192

Fill Your Bible with Life 196

Carve Out Time to Write Together 200

11 SWEETNESS 204

Master a Dessert 206

Savor Every Month 208

Enjoy Afternoon Tea 212

Share the Recipe 214

Just Be Nice 218

12 THE HEART OF SIMPLE HOSPITALITY 222

Remember What is Most Important 224

Your Own Version of Hospitality 226

Don't Let People Go 228

Imperfect Gifts Welcome 232

Share Your Hospitality Ideas With Me 234

About the Author 238

Acknowledgments 241

Dear Reader,

I'm so glad this book has made its way into your hands! This book has been growing in my heart for a very long time. I hope it will help you begin a unique journey that leads you to a more meaningful life!

As you embark on this journey, you will find a collection of simple ideas, or invitations, that are designed to encourage you to see the ordinary as an extraordinary opportunity. I believe there are endless opportunities to make a difference in someone's life, if only we pay a little attention and become aware of the people around us. Every small kindness can make an impact.

This book is a collection of ideas and fun things I have done over the years that hopefully have made a difference for others and created some pleasant memories.

As you begin, remember that you can't do it all. Take one invitation at a time! These ideas are not meant to overwhelm you but rather to spark ideas. Think of them as tools in your toolbox. You don't have to use every tool today! Simply read them and place them in your toolkit for the right time. I have noticed that life offers a variety of seasons. Some seasons provide more time and opportunity for hospitality than others. Give yourself grace and kindness in every season.

How can you use this book? There are so many ways!

You could simply read and gather ideas. You could try one idea per week. You could embark on a hospitality journey by reading this book with friends in a book club or small group setting. One friend shared that she and her daughters selected one idea per week and tried to carry it out. Then, at the end of the week, they shared their experiences with each other.

Implementing this book will look different for each of us, but you, dear reader, can make a difference in the lives of others by showing simple hospitality in your own way.

These 60 ideas or "invitations" are suggestions for you to get started. The goal is for you to become inspired and see how you can come up with your own brand of hospitality.

We have a little garden in our yard, and I love to cut flowers there in the morning. I have noticed that the more flowers I cut, the more flowers bloom. It's good for the plant, and it's good for me, too. As I wander through the garden of life, I cut flowers in the morning and watch the joy bloom as I give them away!

I give away flowers such as kind words, sincere prayers, and notes of encouragement. These simple gestures make a difference as you live a life of fragrant purpose. Will you accept the invitation to add kindness to your everyday life?

CHAPTER ONE

The Mindset of Simple Hospitality

Keep your table set

What do you see when you gaze at your dining room table? I see a blank canvas, ready to paint beautiful moments with friends and family. I see an opportunity to bless neighbors and friends. I see a joyful celebration, and you, dear friend, are invited to the festivities!

"Setting a beautiful table often expresses more love to the family and guests than the food we are about to eat. It shows thoughtfulness and care and attention to details. The simplest meal can be executed with artistry." ~ Luci Swindoll

Keep your table always ready for more than a meal. Keep it set and ready for a delightful moment. After forty years of setting my table, I have gathered a collection of plates, napkins, table runners, and antique silverware, but more than that, I have collected memories that fill my heart with joy.

"Cooking and setting a pretty table makes me feel like I have something to give, something that makes life a little sweeter for other people so that every day wouldn't be like every other." ~ Susan Branch

I am offering that same delight to you with this idea. Whether you are moving into your first apartment, building your family home, or downsizing to a condo at the beach, keep your table always prepared for an unexpected gathering. Your table is an outward display of an inward heart of hospitality. It doesn't take that much to create a beautiful tablescape. No one is impressed by how fancy things are. They will remember how it felt to be there and how nice it was to be invited. The true focus of hospitality is about serving people and making them feel comfortable.

They will remember how it felt to be there and how nice it was to be invited.

"Hospitality" can be defined in many ways, but I define it as "making people feel cared for." Setting your table is one way to prepare to care for those in your life. Anyone who comes into your home is invited to sit down and relax, to laugh and smile, to eat a meal that has been prepared with love. It is excitement on display!

And for me, it is pure joy! I set my table for each season, holiday, or special occasion as a way to look forward to the upcoming fun we will have around the table. I may not know who will walk through the door during a particular season, but I know that I am ready to welcome them.

I want to inspire you to welcome others to your table. If you are prepared, there's a better chance of that happening. I recently ran into a friend whom I had not seen in years. As we caught up, she said, "I have to tell you something. The first time I was in your home fifteen years ago, I noticed your table, beautifully set for Easter. That day was weeks away, but I was overwhelmed by how lovingly it was set." Of course, I appreciated the compliment, but her next remarks were even more important. "I now keep my own table set because of the impression you made on me so many years ago."

Treat your company like family and your family like company.

One of our daughters, Betsy, calls the table "Party ready," and I agree! If you are ready for a party, guess what? You just might host a party any day of the week. Preparing your table is more than an act of decorating for the season. It is preparing your heart to be ready to show hospitality to anyone who walks through your door. Don't just prepare for company. Show your own family they are worth "fussing over," too! Author Rebecca Waters has quoted her mother as saying, "Treat your company like family and your family like company." I like that!

I've always loved to decorate tables. You can see and appreciate beauty in simple things and have unforgettable memories around the table with friends and family. I've always thought of it as a blank canvas where you create something out of nothing, using what you have. Walk out into your yard and see what nature has to offer that day. It can be different each time. I love the saying by Sir Thomas Browne : "Nature is the art of God."

When I think about using what I have to show hospitality, I recall my college dorm room. I loved fixing coffee or tea in my portable hot pot or serving a package of instant soup and crackers for a friend. It doesn't sound like much, but it truly was what I had. It wasn't about the food or that small room that I shared with my roommate. It was about creating a welcoming atmosphere.

When my husband, Scott, and I married, we had a one-bedroom apartment, and we invited a few friends to our new home. Next, it was a townhouse, then a duplex, then a 'real' house. Now, we are enjoying our home on the lake. I love the quote by Socrates: "Contentment is natural wealth." And in each place we've lived, I've found rich contentment in sharing what we have with others.

"To invite a friend to dinner is to become responsible for his [or her] happiness so long as he is under your roof."

A. BRILLAT - SAVARIN, THE FRENCH GASTRONOME

Gifts to go

How ready are you to bless an unexpected person at an unknown time? Hospitality takes a little planning to spark unpredictable joy!

I have always loved finding just the right gifts for people in my life. In Invitation #9, I share more about how I listen for people's interests so that I may collect ideas of special gifts and acts of kindness to give them. I enjoy searching the shelves for that perfect gift, that one that stands out and says, "Choose me!" As much as I love finding a special gift, it's also fun to be on the lookout for sale items to fill your gift closet. It's fun to shop in your own home!

"It isn't what we say or think that defines us, but what we do."

JANE AUSTEN

A gift closet (or drawer or cabinet) is part of the mindset of readiness, and it will allow you to be prepared each time you want to encourage someone in your world. People who come into your life have no idea that you were thinking of them before they wandered in.

Along with gifts, I also keep boxes (and boxes!) of cards and stationery. I keep my eyes open for sales on whimsical or unique gift wrap and gift bags, and I simply hang the gift bags on clothes hangers in my closet, so they are organized, and I can see them easily.

I try to coordinate the gift with the card and the wrapping. It just shows that you put a little extra thought into the gift. Plus, it sure looks nicer!

Recently, our dear friends called and invited my husband, Scott, and me to the beach. The invitation was impromptu because their grandchildren were staying with them for the first part of the week, and we joined them later. I knew just what to do! I went to my gift closet and found a special gift to let this couple know how honored we were to be included in their beach week. I found a book about grandparents and grandchildren along with a Florida candle. I wrapped it in a matching bag with a card, and we were off to the beach! It's always nice to be prepared. The act of being able to quickly choose a gift and a card was stress free, because I had prepared ahead of time.

Hospitality takes a little planning to spark unpredictable joy!

Encouragement with a card

Plato reportedly said, "Be kind, for everyone you meet is fighting a hard battle." We read verification of this in John 16:33, where it says, "In this world, you will have trouble."

We are certain that people we know are encountering difficulties in various areas of their lives. From stress at work, at home, or even in their own minds, our friends are fighting battles of some sort, big or small.

I have found that a note of encouragement goes a long way, but if I am not ready to give encouragement, I might let an opportunity slip away. So, I have a drawer full of uplifting cards at my fingertips. Do not underestimate the power of your kind words. Simple words of encouragement are gifts we can all give without cost. A genuine compliment, a sincere apology, a heartfelt thank you—all these are soothing to the soul. Sharing these words costs so little, but it can make all the difference in the world to someone having a bad day.

First, keep your eyes open for beautiful cards, notecards, and stationery so you have a variety of cards to suit anyone. The card is just the beginning! Also, you could keep a stash of different stamps so you can find the right one for each card. I keep my stamps in a three-ring binder with plastic sleeves, an idea I garnered from the post office years ago. Stamps cost the same, so you might as well try and use a good one! Plus, it shows you put a little extra thought into what you are sending them. I order stamps online from the post office (usps.com), and it's as easy as can be! If you receive a card from me, know that I have chosen the stamp . . . just for you! Handwritten cards are the grace notes of life! They make people happy and show your love.

Handwritten cards are the grace notes of life!

I like to always add something special to the card, such as pressed flowers or leaves, a recipe, a prayer card, a Bible verse, or even a pretty paper napkin. I sometimes mail snippets of memories, a photo or some little memento that can fit inside the card. When the whole package you send is intentional, your encouragement means even more. Like the Latin proverb that says, "The word that is heard perishes, but the letter that is written remains."

If you just keep your eyes and ears open, you will see and hear of opportunities in which you have a chance to make a small, but hopefully encouraging difference in the lives of people who come across your path. The international sign to know if someone needs encouragement is if they are breathing. If they are breathing, they need encouragement." said S. Truett Cathy, founder of Chick-fil-A.

My goal is to brighten the world, one note at a time. I want to write truly heartfelt words. Each little package of love reminds the receiver that someone really cares about them. I want the person who opens my card to know that I took time to send them something special, which is a way to show your love. Most of us don't realize the impact our small gestures of kindness can have on others. A handwritten note is like a hug in an envelope. We can love people with the simple power of a handwritten note. We all have a chance to leave a mark on someone's heart today. I know words are powerful, and I want to use mine well. As you read this, is there someone who comes to mind that you could send a note of encouragement to this week?

"Do small things with great love."
MOTHER THERESA

The foundation of hospitality is the desire to show love in everything you do. Mother Theresa said, "Do small things with great love." Simple hospitality is following this advice.

It is my goal to brighten the world, one note at a time.

I am always looking for cards on sale. I look at Hallmark, Home Goods, the Rifle Paper Company in Winter Park, Florida, and even Dollar Tree (they have beautiful cards for $0.50 or $1). I love it when our grocery store has a buy one/get one free offer on cards. If you find a good price, you can send more!

I even like to purchase cards on sale for our daughters, Betsy and Anna. They love to send cards too, but being busy young mothers, they don't have much time to go out shopping for them. It's a double blessing to give cards to them because it extends my love for the written word. There's joy in letter writing for both the writer and the receiver.

Recently, I met with a mom who expressed an interest in my stamp collection. She wanted to begin sending special cards with beautiful stamps but was not sure where to begin. I thought I could start a collection for her. I gathered some of my favorite stamps, some that would represent her well, and I gave them to her, placed right on the card, ready to send on an array of cards.

You can encourage others too. You don't need a special stamp collection, but it's a fun way to be ready!

Bring the fragrance of flowers

I love the fragrance of flowers. Claude Monet said, "I must have flowers always and always." I agree! The smell of roses or magnolias can bring something special to any setting. When we smell a fragrant flower, we are delighted! Maybe that is why the Bible calls us to be "the fragrance of Christ." We are to bring life and joy to those we encounter.

I recall a Bible study many years ago in which we studied the fragrance of Christ, and as we studied, I took a deep breath. Orange blossoms. It was a scent I won't forget, as it added to the beauty of the study that day. We had three orange trees in our yard, and it was so easy to cut them and bring the blossoms to share with friends.

We are to bring life and joy to those we encounter.

One day, not too long ago, I was expecting a less than beautiful day. I needed to get the COVID-19 vaccine and had already heard about long lines of people waiting in their cars. I could not stop thinking about the nurses and frontline workers who were working long shifts, in the hot Florida sun, to serve us. It was very last minute, but as I went out the door, I cut some pink camellias and drove to my vaccination site. Unfortunately, not everyone came to the line with flowers and a good attitude. I do recall one driver in the line honking and yelling at me because he thought I was in his way, and I just looked at my camellias on the seat next to me and took a deep breath. He was not in a good state of mind, but I was determined to bless someone that day.

I waited three and half hours, and when I gave the flowers and my note of thanks to the nurses who helped me, they truly seemed touched. One nurse said, "No one has done anything like this." We shared a smile and a happy moment, and I said a quiet prayer for her.

I am convinced that flowers can elevate any moment. They bring joy and they elicit memories.

We recently had our home repainted, and the men painting were doing a fantastic job. I wanted to thank them, to elevate their day and let them know that they were doing excellent work and that we truly appreciated them.

So, I set up a little card table on our front porch with a fresh flower, bottles of cold water and a plate of brownies. I was almost embarrassed by the whole spread; I wasn't sure what they would think. I almost didn't do it! But when I did, they were so pleased. One of them took a few photos and sent them to his wife. He told me the same thing the nurse had said, "No one has ever done this for us." I told him, "Well . . . I hope it's not the last!" Kindness can be brave; it can be stepping out of your comfort zone to do something for others that you maybe haven't done before.

Whether you are picking up lab results, returning a library book, or picking up children from school, any situation can be elevated with the beauty of flowers and a kind word of thanks.

Kindness can be brave; it can be stepping out of your comfort zone to do something for others that you maybe haven't done before.

Offer what you have

My dear friend Molly and I have served together for many years. We volunteer at our local hospital every Thursday on the chemotherapy floor. We serve tea in beautiful teacups at the same time each week. Some of the patients even schedule their chemo on Thursdays to be a part of the teatime. It's something nice the hospital offers for the patient and family members during a very difficult time.

I love the sound of the tea cart as it rattles down the hall. The sound signifies that someone is coming to bring something special and a listening ear to anyone who needs it. I have noticed over the years that some people are very quiet and contemplative during chemotherapy. A smile and a warm drink are enough.

Others want to talk. I try to be available and offer whatever I can. One patient stands out to me. She was there alone, and she told me all about her life and family; we had a special connection.

When I handed her the delicate cobalt blue and gold china teacup, she remarked, "Oh, this cup is from Russia, and I am from Russia!" She seemed so delighted by the beauty of it! Something in my heart just wanted her to keep that cup. I said, "I want you to have this."

I could see in her eyes that it meant a lot to her.

The mindset of being available to people can change the way you experience a normal day. Any day can be special when you listen carefully and look for ways to give of yourself to others.

Any day can be special when you listen carefully and look for ways to give of yourself to others.

1) When you hear the word, "Hospitality," what comes to mind?

2) Can you recall a time when someone sparked unexpected joy in your life?

3) What people came to mind as you read about the mindset of simple hospitality?

4) What comes to your mind when you read that, "Everyone is fighting a battle?" How does that encourage you to add kindness to your every day life?

5) What idea most resonated with you this week?

CHAPTER TWO

Give the Gift of Kindness

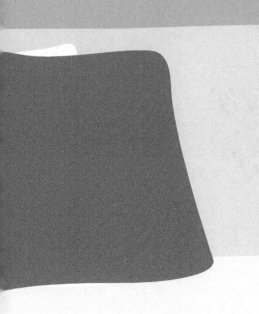

Make your home the headquarters of kindness

The foundation of a good "thank you" is a heart of appreciation. My goal is to make our home a place of kindness, a place of hospitality. Kindness begins and ends at home. It is truly one of the greatest gifts you can give to someone. Anyone who comes inside or around our home can be touched by kindness. A kind word is never wasted. We all have a chance to make an impression on someone, even if it is just for a few moments. Our lives speak louder than our words. What is your life saying to others? Arnold Palmer always said: "Whatever you do in your life, turn the table over and treat others like you want to be treated when you're on the other side." It's not too hard nor is it too late.

A kind word is never wasted.

If we hire someone to repair, service, or enter our home, I want that person to know that we appreciate the work he or she is doing. I might be baking a treat as they begin so the cookies have cooled and are ready to eat by the time they finish their work. I have also cut flowers and given them to the men who are working so they can take those flowers to their wives, mothers, friends, or just keep them to enjoy!

However, these moments of inspiration would not come if I had not made up my mind many years ago that our home would be used for this purpose. It is not just walls and carpet and a roof. Our house is not only here for our personal enjoyment. I want it to be a place of kindness. As a mother, I have learned the power to create the kind of home I want my children to remember.

I have always tried to be intentional and not waste small moments to teach big things.

My husband and I have raised three children: Betsy, Michael, and Anna. I have always tried to be intentional and not waste small moments to teach big lessons. A friend, Miriam was telling me a story that I just loved. A child she encountered must have been learning about kindness. That little four-year-old came up to her and asked the simple question, "What have you done that is *kind* today?" Good food for thought, isn't it? Most of us desire to connect with others. When we do so, this brings us a feeling of joy and satisfaction. We feel happiness and pleasure when we give to others. Little children do, too.

One day I was chatting with the woman who delivers our mail. She saw that I was receiving a birthday card, and she remarked that she has a birthday close to the same time. That little piece of information was just what I needed! I now knew that her birthday was coming up. The next day, I left a card in the mailbox for her. She seemed truly touched! She said, "No one has ever done this for me." I told her that I was so happy she liked it, and that story still makes me smile. As I look for ways to thank people, bless others, and bring a little sunshine into the lives around my home, my life becomes richer. The relationships that develop around the house—with neighbors, service providers, and the people who roll in and out of our lives—become sweeter. Kindness only grows. As you extend kindness from your home, you will be enriched at each turn. May every day you live make a difference for someone.

I sincerely hope that anyone who has entered our house will have good memories when they drive by, and think to themselves, "There was just *something* about that house . . ."

Do all the good you can
by all the means you can
in all the ways you can
in all the places you can
to all the people you can
as long as you can.

JOHN WESLEY

*Traveling
kindness*

Once you have established your home as a place of kindness, it's time to take that on the road. Be on the lookout to be kind, even if you don't have a plan. You cannot do it for everyone, but you can do it for someone.

A couple years ago, my brother, Jim, and his family had a layover at the Orlando airport, not too far from our home. We wanted to see them, so I was trying to think how I could make it memorable. It was February, when the strawberries are in season in Florida, so I made a fresh strawberry pie, and we traveled to the airport with it. We took along plates and forks and had a party right there in the middle of Terminal A! It was memorable, for sure!

Deep Dish Strawberry Pie

Deep dish pie shell
1 quart strawberries
2/3 c. sugar
1 c. cold water

3T. cornstarch
1 small package strawberry Jell-o

Bake and cool a deep dish pie shell. Slice strawberries and arrange in a pie shell. mix together in sauce pan sugar, water and cornstarch. Bring to a boil, stirring occasionally. Cook sauce until thick and glossy. Won't take long. Add 1 small package of Jello. Stir well. Take off heat and cool. Pour over fruit. Refrigerate. Serve with whipped cream. Enjoy! ♡

I have always enjoyed making bread. I do it the easy way, with an electric bread maker. I make a loaf, and hop into the car with the warm, fresh loaf in my front seat. Then I ask God, "Who do you want me to bless today?" Sometimes I will also have a copy of *Our Daily Bread*, one of my favorite devotional publications, with me to complete the gift, along with a short note. The bread will soon be gone, but the note and devotional will be something tangible for the person to keep, at least for a little while.

Kindness is something we can all practice daily.

Many times, when our children were small and in the car with me as I went about my day, we would look for someone with whom we could share our loaf of bread. From a neighbor to a teacher to the family we carpool with, there's always someone to receive what you have to give.

Traveling kindness does not always involve a random act of kindness, though. I try to listen and find out when friends or family members are sick. I know how bad it feels to be under the weather, and I try to bring what I would like when I'm not feeling well. One day, I learned that my friend Sara and her entire family were sick. I packed up some soup, crackers, and soda, along with a pretty card, and simply left these goodies at their front door. It doesn't take that much to make someone's day or to let them know that you are thinking of them. When those things are available, you can just grab them, pack them, and deliver! It's kindness in the form of a care package. Kindness will look different for everyone.

One added benefit to taking others along as you spread kindness is that you can teach them how to do the same. I am often brought to tears as I hear about our children or grandchildren spreading kindness. They have caught the bug, and I am so proud of them! Kindness is contagious, so find ways to spread it as often as you can. In all the places we go throughout our day, we all have a choice. What kind of difference will you make in another person's life?

Kindness is contagious, so find ways to spread it as often as you can.

I love how our oldest daughter has embraced teaching her children about the importance of learning someone's name and being kind to others. Using someone's name is like music to their ears. They have a wonderful garbage man in their neighborhood named, Orville. Connor and Will are five and three years old, and they love the sound of the green garbage truck coming down their street on Tuesdays. Betsy has helped the boys draw pictures for Orville, and he proudly has them taped inside his garbage truck. Don't you just love that?

Kindness is something we can all practice daily. What *kind* thing have you done today?

Creative kindness

In friendship and in life, a quality I am drawn to is *kindness*. Kindness in a person makes me relax and feel comfortable. I want to offer that to others.

Aesop wrote, "No act of kindness, no matter how small, is ever wasted." Opportunities for kindness are everywhere if you look and if you are willing to be a little bit creative.

What situation is in front of you? What do you have to share? Who is around you? What is happening in their lives? It takes a little bit of time to stop and think, but it's undoubtedly worth the effort. Why don't you make the choice to live with your eyes wide open to really *see* people?

I believe it's best to live your life with faithfulness and to be committed to the small, important things that we can tend to overlook in the quest to do something grand with our lives. It's easy to somehow miss the fact that the small things can ultimately end up being the biggest things.

For example, I might have some extra chili that I have made. Rather than freeze it, I think, "Who might like some chili?" I might send it home with a service person or a friend who stopped by. I may text a neighbor to see if he or she would like it for dinner. Years ago, my neighbor and I would occasionally share what we were having for dinner that night. Someone else's cooking always tastes better, right?

If I am slicing watermelon, and I have too much for our family, I take some slices to a family with young children. I have a memory of a dreadfully hot Florida day when our air conditioner wasn't working, and I was thankful I could offer that repairman sliced, ice-cold watermelon. There are endless ways to brighten the day of people in your life; ways that don't have to cost much money or take a lot of time.

I remember one evening I had made homemade soup, and we had enough for another family. My friend Terri's father had been in the hospital, and I could tell she was discouraged. When I called her and offered to bring her family dinner, spur of the moment, she said, "Oh, we are already in our pajamas!" I told our children to put on their PJs, and off we went to deliver the meal. I did that crazy thing because I wanted our friends to feel comfortable. Everyone was in pajamas, and it was a great memory!

In my carpooling days, I loved surprising my friend Shugie or her husband, JB, with a cup of morning coffee. They would return the coffee mug at the end of the school day. It was a regular drive-thru coffee shop at our house. Frances Hodgson Burnette wrote, "It is astonishing how short a time it takes for very wonderful things to happen." Morning coffee is pretty wonderful, isn't it?

I have been on the receiving end of a special meal, too. Last Christmas Eve, Scott's sister, Lori, and her husband, Mark, gave us the gift of our traditional (as in years and years!) dinner to be delivered to our front door. We were not feeling well and were so sad to not be joining them for Christmas Eve that year. How special to have the same meal we always ate together, even though we were apart. We're fortunate in Florida that we can sit outdoors in December. I had a fresh flower centerpiece on our card table, which was covered with a tablecloth—complete with our Christmas china and candles burning. We weren't as sad since we were sharing the traditional meal, even though we couldn't be together.

This Christmas I was given a beautiful gift from our soon-to-be daughter-in-law, Ashley Rowley. She had secretly gotten a letter from my sister, Jeana that contained a beloved recipe for apple pie. Ashley found a company to imprint this on a tea towel in my grandmother's handwriting from forty years earlier. There were tears as her words came to life! What an example of creative, loving kindness. She also made a photo album from the day our son Michael asked her to be his wife, and included a letter thanking me for being Michael's mom and raising such a fine son. Ashley is a very special young woman and we can't wait for her to officially be our daughter-in-law!

Using creativity and your own personal touch is what makes these moments memorable and special. The way *you* deliver kindness will be different than the way I deliver it. I like to keep magazine articles I find that describe places I would like to visit. I love to be ready for a trip! I keep those articles in a filing cabinet, and when my husband and I travel, I pull them out for reference. One thing I love to do is to bring the article to the owner of a place. Recently, we visited the historic Woodstock Inn in Vermont. I had cut out an article thirty-two years earlier from the travel section of our *Orlando Sentinel* newspaper. It's fun to be ready with ideas for a trip and share them with others too. As you use your creative spirit, you will find life sweeter, richer, and more delightful!

Listen with intention

The first step in loving people well is listening well. If you really listen, people will tell you things that can give clues as to ways you could love them and special ways to be kind to them specifically. They share needs, wants, concerns, and desires. They reveal little pieces of their heart, and it's up to you what to do with that revelation. Will you seize the opportunity to deliver your special brand of kindness?

I believe you can share kindness with anyone, anytime. If you look hard, you can see people. You can hear them. It's a beautiful gift to try and notice those in your life. Most people like to talk about themselves and notice when someone is interested. I love to say to people, "Tell me your story."

I remember the point in my life when I decided to treat everyone equally. At the time, I had two jobs. It was 1979, and I had begun my career as a dental hygienist. However, I still held onto my part-time job as a waitress at Dayton's Department store in Minneapolis. I noticed that people treated me differently when I was in my role as a hygienist. I saw and experienced for myself that we were not all equal in other people's eyes. They treated me with just a little bit more respect. They showed me a little more appreciation and spoke to me with a different tone because I was a professional. They noticed my name and made a point to learn a little bit about me.

> *"The first step in loving people well is listening well."*

However, in my role as a waitress, people treated me differently. I never understood this. I was still me. I was the same person; I just wore a different uniform. But the people who interacted with me on a regular basis did not always treat me as well.

I decided back then that I would always treat people with the same level of dignity and respect. I especially like to make a point to thank people I see cleaning the restroom. It can be a difficult and thankless job. I try to make a point to smile and say, "Thank you." A sweet lady named Daisy works at a favorite place of ours called Oxford Exchange in Tampa. It's a wonderful restaurant, bookstore, coffeehouse, and gift shop. I always look for Daisy whenever we are there. Her smile is such a day brightener. I know not everyone talks to the people who clean restrooms, but she's such a delight, and I love to tell her, "Thank you."

One thing I enjoy doing is listening to our server when we go out to eat and trying to hear a way that I can surprise him or her. Betty, who had become a friend, told us that she had lost eighty pounds, so the next day, I mailed a card to her workplace telling her, "Congratulations!" What an amazing accomplishment worth acknowledging!

I like to cut flowers from our yard and take them to people whenever I can. The woman who cuts my hair, Candy, loves roses, so I try to take her roses when they are in bloom. Sometimes, I will just snap a picture of the roses and text, "Thinking of you."

I have learned that flowers are "One size fits all!" Whether the camellias are blooming, or the azaleas are in season, no one will turn down flowers because they just don't fit.

My neighbor Brenda told me once that she liked my roses. I thought it might be nice to cut some roses and leave them at the end of her driveway for her to enjoy while she and her husband went for a walk. In return, she surprised me and left orchids at my front door. From those small kindnesses, something happened. We invited Brenda and her husband, Toby, to sit on our front porch one night as we enjoyed some appetizers, and three hours later, all four of us felt like friends. Although we had been waving to those neighbors for years, we had never really gotten to know one another. The simple act of listening and a small act of kindness started a new friendship.

New friends are all around you! You just have to pay attention!

Opportunities for kindness are everywhere if you listen with intention. Listen to people with the desire to bless them. This day will never come again. What will you do with it? Sometimes we can over complicate our desire to make a difference, and then our good intentions go no further. Choose something simple you can follow through with that will encourage you to do more. That will build your confidence and encourage you to do something else for someone.

Our thoughts are the beginning of action. One of my favorite verses is Philippians 4:8 (NIV), which reads, "Whatever is true, whatever is noble, whatever is right, whatever is pure, whatever is lovely, whatever is admirable—if anything is excellent or praiseworthy—think about such things." We become what we think.

Listening and showing kindness does not always include a present or card, though. When you listen closely, you may find that someone just needs a word of encouragement or a compliment, even in the grocery store! I have always thought, "When you think a kind thing about a person, go ahead and say it!" That compliment belongs to the person. It shouldn't just stay in your mind. There is no reason to keep that to yourself! I love Mark Twain's statement, "I can live

Whatever is true, whatever is noble, whatever is right, whatever is pure, whatever is lovely, whatever is admirable— if anything is excellent or praiseworthy—think about such things.

for two months on a good compliment." If you notice something positive about someone, just say it! If you see a person who needs a kind word, don't hold back. I especially look for young moms or older people who might need a tender word of encouragement. We all could use a kind word in our day. Compliment someone and mean it!

One day, I was at the grocery store, and a most beautiful silver-haired lady was shopping. I finally couldn't help myself and said, "You are just so beautiful!" She smiled and said, "Thank you, honey," and proceeded to say, "Do you always shop on Thursdays, too?" Honestly, I have no idea when I shop, but I loved that she was hoping for connection. I'm so glad I went for it when I felt prompted to remind her of her beauty. Although it takes a little courage, saying something is always worth it.

Kindness and gratitude

Gratitude and kindness go perfectly together. I love to look for ways to thank people with a special touch of kindness behind the thank you note. I believe there is importance in a sincere and heartfelt thank you.

A few years ago, I underwent reconstructive surgery on my ankle. It was a big surgery with a long recovery, and the doctor who performed the surgery did an incredible job. I felt such gratitude and kept looking for the right way to thank him. I brought him a homemade treat for my last appointment because I wanted to let him and his staff know I appreciated the care they had given me. But when the Junior League 5K came around, I saw a way to really let him know what he meant to me. I walked with my husband in the race and then brought my race bib back to my doctor. He was a dedicated runner himself, and it was a way I could truly thank him. I was able to show him wholehearted kindness because I was full of gratitude for what he had done for me.

I also like to let my heart fill with gratitude when I use something that someone I love has given to me. My sweet friend Carrie gave me a beautiful Spode blue and white teapot for a special birthday gift. I used it this week, and I snapped a picture, texted it to her, and just said, "Thinking of you!" If someone comes to mind, I try to let them know. I always love when I hear from someone and they tell me they are thinking of me, don't you?

Kindness is something we can all practice daily.

Luci Swindoll was the author in a book titled, *Extravagant Grace,* where she encouraged readers to look for grace in every area of life. I agree, and I would add to look for ways to show extravagant gratitude. Showing gratitude starts by noticing people rather than overlooking them, by taking time to appreciate people at unexpected times.

I often will be spending time with a friend or witnessing a kind act, and I will think, "I cannot wait to get home and write the thank you note." I know some people struggle with this, but I have true excitement when I get to send a thank you note. There is a certain magic in a handwritten note. They are so rare these days. It is truly a joy to find the perfect way to thank someone for a kindness they have shown me or for a job well done. It doesn't have to be expensive or take a lot of time. It simply must come from the heart.

Teach your children to write thank you notes as well. "Unexpressed gratitude communicates ingratitude," is what I have heard pastor and author Andy Stanley say. If you want to stand out above the rest, simply write them. When our children were young and got a check as a gift, I didn't let them cash it until they wrote the note. A handwritten thank you is an act of love. It's a way to properly honor the person who spent precious time or money on you. It can be very short, but I encourage you to just write it.

Colossians 3:12 tells us, "Clothe yourself with compassion, kindness, and gentleness." We need that in our world today more than ever!

1) What smells remind you of your childhood home?

2) Do you agree that kindness is contagious? Explain.

3) Share a creative idea you have had with this group.

4) Can you think of someone who listens well? What did he or she do that made you feel heard?

5) What idea most resonated with you this week?

CHAPTER THREE

The Written Word

Send a gift through special words

A word of encouragement is often just the gift a person needs to feel loved. Sending a note of encouragement is like documenting and solidifying the fact that a person is worthy of love. Phone calls are nice but a letter or card is forever. Not only is letter writing part of my weekly routine, but it is also a beautiful ritual that I look forward to. I enjoy crafting the right words, finding the perfect card, and even finishing it all with a matching stamp to let someone know that he or she is special to me. When someone opens a letter from me, I hope that they feel important.

A word of encouragement is often just the gift a person needs to feel loved.

Once again, sending a note of encouragement or a written gift of encouragement mainly begins with having an open ear and an open heart. As I set about my day, I listen for opportunities of encouraging someone who may be entering a new phase of life or needing a little extra attention. Recently, a friend, Natalie, mentioned that her daughter was leaving that Thursday for France to be an au pair. So on that Tuesday, I placed a card in the mail to Natalie because I knew that it would be tough to send her daughter across the ocean. Even though I knew she was happy for the adventure her daughter was embarking upon, I anticipated that she might be feeling a little anxious. She and her daughter are very close, and this is a big move!

It was time to go shopping, but not in a store. I opened a drawer in the bedroom closet with boxes of cards for every occasion. I searched for something special, a card to fit the moment. I was delighted to find a card with the word, "Bonjour" on the front! I knew it was a serendipitous moment, and it was fun to seize it. After writing a few lines of encouragement and adding a special stamp, my gift of a card was complete.

A few days later, I received a call from my dear friend. We talked about how she was feeling, and we had a moment to connect. She appreciated the fact that I was thinking about her. There's nothing like encouraging your friend when it comes to their children. I know that always means so much to me.

A word of encouragement in the form of a letter is often the spark to deepen relationships. If you do not know someone very well, this type of communication can help you get to know him or her better. If you are already good friends, it rekindles or strengthens the friendship.

By taking time to choose lovely words and send cheery cards or a kind word on personalized stationery, you will make your own life sweeter. It's something you will never regret.

Create a
lovely system

Birthdays and anniversaries have always been important to me. I remember seeing my mother and grandmother write down important dates in their "birthday book," and I think it was ingrained in me from an early age to celebrate the people we love on days that are special to them. As I leaf through my own birthday book, filled with dates of family members and close friends, I can't help but smile. I enjoy seeing their names, written in my own handwriting. I treasure what each date means to me, my husband, and to our children. Although you can certainly keep up with important dates in a digital calendar, I have treasured keeping a handwritten one that has stood the test of time. In fact, my grandmother gave me this birthday book before I was married over forty years ago. The book still has my maiden name on the first page!

Often, when I speak to young women about celebrating birthdays, they remark, "Jennifer, I *want* to send birthday cards. I just cannot seem to remember." Most people are not lacking in a desire to send birthday and anniversary cards. Rather, they lack having an enjoyable system that allows the process to be a beautiful and easy experience.

What works for me is having cards on hand in the first place. Although I purchase special cards for my family, I try to keep a variety of birthday cards and anniversary cards organized in a drawer, so they are easily accessible. Whenever I see a beautiful card or a sale on stationery, I try to add it to my collection. I try to keep all my cards organized so they are easy to find. Waiting until a birthday sneaks up on you creates stress. My goal is for this whole process to be joyful, not stressful. Phyllis Theroux said, "To send a letter is a good way to go somewhere without moving anything but your heart."

I love to give my friends or family the makings of a cup of birthday tea. With tears in her eyes, my dental hygienist, Kimberly, said, "You always remember my birthday. You send a beautiful card with tea and a napkin. You remember me!" As a little girl, I had a paper napkin collection, and I guess my love for them just carried into adulthood. It's an easy addition that fits inside an envelope.

During the last week of each month, I open my birthday book and make a list of the days to celebrate. Using my list, I try to choose the perfect card for each person who has a special day in the coming month. Rather than writing cards throughout the month, I take about an hour and write every card in advance, signing them and sealing them. Then, I place them in an ordered stack, ready to mail. I try to mail them so that they will arrive early, a day or two before the birthday or anniversary.

I have learned that it takes a little bit of planning, but the preparation makes the habit more fun. My advice is, "Never write one birthday card." If you are buying one card, go ahead and buy a few more. If you are writing a single birthday card, look ahead and write a few more. Stamp them. Place the cards where you will see them. This will give you that wonderful feeling of being prepared for the next special event in your loved ones' lives.

> *"To send a letter is a good way to go somewhere without moving anything but your heart."*
>
> PHYLLIS THEROUX

A while back, my husband asked me how many cards I had sent. When I told him I had no idea, I decided to start keeping track, just for the fun of it! I was absolutely shocked to learn that I had mailed out 3,149 cards or letters in the past eight-and-a-half years. That ends up being about one card a day. I guess that *is* a lot!

I had an experience that I won't soon forget. I was sitting at the computer one day, and I saw something pop up on my screen. I read about a teacher from Indiana who sent birthday cards each year to students he had in his class, not just that particular year, but even after they moved on. I sat there, alone in front of the computer in our sun room, and just teared up at the thought of this dedicated teacher committing to stay in touch each year with his students. That was several years ago, and it seems like yesterday. I can put myself back there at any time. I was so touched by his act of generosity. He not only sent a card but included a personal letter. I just feel that it's important to stay in touch with people. Maybe because that's part of the reason I believe I am here . . . that's part of my contribution in a person's life; for them to be remembered.

An unexpected note

-

I keep my soul alive by letter writing. I try to write truly heartfelt notes. As much as I love sending birthday cards, I think I enjoy sending unexpected notes even more! My children, grandchildren, and friends have come to expect a card or gift on their birthday, but sending a card on a surprising day brings immense joy. It's fun for me, and it's fun for the receiver.

This can mean sending cards on a smaller holiday like Valentine's Day or Mother's Day. I try to switch up the holidays that I send cards. It can mean sending a note of encouragement to someone who doesn't normally receive a letter from you. It can also mean dropping a note of thanks to someone who has given great service at a restaurant. I even enjoy sending cards to my friends' children at camp or college or sending notes to my friends' parents when they are ill or need a special touch.

I discovered this joy the year our daughters got married. Both daughters married within just 18 months of each other. Since the family was more focused on two weddings and all the festivities around those special days, I was not thinking about sending Christmas cards that year. Instead, we sent our friends and family a Valentine's Day card with photos from both weddings. I have never gotten so many comments! The unexpected part made it more fun, and I knew I had found a new way to bring a smile to the faces of friends. Everyone deserves to get something other than a bill in the mail every once in a while!

This year, I sent a great deal of Mother's Day cards to family and friends. I don't always do that. I know . . . it's kind of crazy how I just love Mother's Day. I am truly surrounded by some incredible mothers, and it was my pleasure to celebrate them and let them know that they are doing a great job. I love that there is a special day each year that is set aside to honor motherhood.

I keep my soul alive by letter writing.

Other great card moments might include Easter and Thanksgiving Day. As you search for special moments to celebrate, you can also think outside the calendar. You can send cards to commemorate beautiful events that only you can see. One of my dear friend's sons recently got married. I saw her and noticed the most beautiful glow on her face! She looked absolutely radiant, and I could not wait to send her a note to let her know how gorgeous she was, and retell my favorite moments of the wedding day. That lets the day live on for both of us.

If you have grandchildren or children in your life, try to regularly put a note or card in the mail to them. Kids love getting something in their mailbox. I have met our little grandson's mailman, who they affectionately call, "Mailman Larry," and he is just who you would imagine in your mind's eye to be the neighborhood mail deliverer. I love being on the lookout for something to send our grandchildren. My mom was so good at sending comics or other fun things such as stickers in the mail to our kids as they were growing up. We went blueberry picking with the little boys last year, and I was so happy I actually had a blueberry stamp that I had saved from long ago. It's all about the small things, right? They love firetrucks and construction equipment, and whenever I can find a reason to mail them something, I do. I want them to love the mail, too.

Part of the reason I love to send unexpected cards is because I know so much of our mail can be uneventful. I love breaking through the mundane routines and bringing a friend a little sunshine. You have an opportunity to bring light into the lives of people around you all day. Each word of encouragement is a ray that warms the heart of the people in your life.

Add a special surprise

When someone walks to the mailbox and discovers a personal note from you, how does that person feel? It's likely that they will open your letter first. I know that I quickly look over the mail that I receive each day to find the personalized mail, and I open that one first. Or, sometimes I "save the best for last!" Why? The mail from friends brings a smile to my face! I want each letter that I send to invoke an honest smile in the receiver.

My favorite way to send a smile-worthy note is to add a special surprise such as a tea bag or pretty napkin. Rather than only opening a letter, they are discovering a special package unlike any other letter they will pull out of their mailbox. Hopefully it will be the one they will remember and will continue to bring a smile to their face. Why do I do that? I love taking a few minutes to stop and "take time for tea." It's not so much the tea, but what it can represent is just pausing in the day for a few minutes.

I have a friend, Lauri, in New York who always sends me a tea bag as well. We have a little shared memory that continues to bring us both joy. Sending a special surprise creates a sweet memory between the two of us. That is why I have a drawer of teas from around the world and napkins that I have collected over the years. Alexandra Stoddard wrote, "The correct word is like any small detail—it enhances life." I feel the same way about the right surprise inside a card. It enhances the experience.

How can you elevate the experience for the person who is receiving the card?

How can you elevate the experience for the person who is receiving the card? What can you add to help it stand out?

Another collection I enjoy is an assortment of lovely prayer cards. I love to say a special prayer for people in my life. Even as I walk through the neighborhood, sometimes, I pray for people in the homes I pass. A prayer is a word of encouragement that can change the hearts and lives of everyone around you. By choosing a unique prayer card for your reader, you can show your friends how much you are thinking of them.

May your writing ritual bring joy from every angle! It is something that can be pleasant and memorable for you, and it sends joy to the recipient. I hope that you create a letter-writing habit that enriches your life and builds deeper relationships. I never consider words of encouragement as a duty or a task on my list. It is a delight to send a special memory in the mail.

Letters
to authors

I love books. There are so many books! Reading is dreaming while you are wide awake! I never knew there was a name for someone who is a lover of books. He or she is called a bibliophile. I guess I qualify because I certainly do love books! It's wonderful to cuddle up with a book, don't you think? No one has ever cuddled up to a website. At times, I think people are getting tired of everything digital. Most people want to be able to sit down in comfort and look through a book in person. I like the way they feel in my hand and the way they warm my heart. Each book in my personal library has not only opened my eyes but has also shaped the way I go about my day. Whenever I buy a new book, I place a return address label inside the cover along with the date in case someone borrows it or finds it—or in case I find it years later and wonder when it came into my life.

I recently opened my signed copy of Alexandra Stoddard's book, *Living a Beautiful Life*, and as I leafed through the pages, I smiled, thinking of the thirty beautiful years that had passed since I purchased it. As I look around my home, I realize that I took a lot of her advice. Her ideas spoke to me when we first established our home and even now, all those years later, I see their influence. I truly feel grateful for the lovely way she wrote her book and how it impacted my life.

When authors speak to me, I love to speak back. One of my joys is writing to authors to let them know what they mean to me. As I read through the book again, I see on the final page that she "welcomes messages from her readers." She is in her early 80's now, and I think she would enjoy knowing that ideas from her book are sprinkled throughout my home. She gave me insight, courage, and inspiration that has grown in my heart over the years. Why not let her know? Recently, I wrote to Alexandra Stoddard and sent a photocopy of what she had signed when I had bought her book. I also included a picture I took of her and her husband at the bookstore in Mount Dora where she had spoken at a book signing. It was a lovely surprise to find a letter back from her in my mailbox!

Another author who has heavily influenced me is Susan Branch. I wrote to her many years ago and shared what her book meant to me. I imagine

> *"I still find each day too short for all the thoughts I want to think, all the walks I want to take, all the books I want to read, and all the friends I want to see."*
>
> JOHN BURROUGHS

that authors must pour their hearts into whatever they write, so why not let them know it was worth all of that hard work? I still have the letter Susan wrote back on her personal stationery, taped to the inside cover of one of her books.

One other author I have been thinking about lately is Luci Swindoll. She is the sister of Pastor Chuck Swindoll, and she was a fantastic author. Her book, *You Bring the Confetti*, was one of my personal favorites. She loved life and found great joy in celebrating every day. We were similar in that way.

She wrote, "A life of adventure is ours for the taking, whether we're seven or seventy. Life for the most part is what you make it. We have been given a responsibility to live it fully, joyfully, completely, and richly, in whatever span of time God grants us on this earth."

I am so grateful that she put those words down on paper because she gave me a vision to live life like an adventure. I actually met Luci Swindoll once on a cruise that my husband and I had the chance to go on. She signed a copy of her book, and I got to tell her how much I appreciated her.

However, now, I want to send a letter to her brother, Chuck Swindoll, who is a pastor and well-known writer himself. Since Luci passed away last year, I imagine he would enjoy getting a letter to let him know that his sister was special to me. I am sure she still lives in his heart as she does in mine. I am going to make sure he knows that.

Jan Karon is another favorite author to whom I have written. I had a chance to visit her recently opened museum in the small town of Hudson, NC. She says, "If you love people, they will love you back." I believe that! There is a gift shop there called "Happy Endings," which contains many of her books. Doesn't the name just make you smile?

I always thought that, if I ever had a chance to write a book, I would love to hear that some of the thoughts and ideas I shared made a difference for readers.

1) What link do you see between kindness and gratitude?

2) What are some ways to cheer on another person as they try something new or go through a difficult time?

3) When has someone encouraged you? What did he or she say that was so memorable?

4) Share an idea of a special surprise inside a letter!

CHAPTER FOUR

Take Hospitality on the Road

Tea party to go

As a young mother, I had the privilege of meeting regularly with an older woman named Joy Torell. Joy had grown children and grandchildren, and she was gracious enough to take time to mentor me. This was before the word "mentor" was even a common word. She poured into me by sharing her favorite books and favorite scriptures with me. I would drop our little Betsy at Mom's Day Out, and off I would go to Joy's house.

Each week, I looked forward to my time with Joy. I was always impressed that she set the table for me. For me . . . just me! She always had a beautiful tea set with piping hot water ready for us. She often made us lemon squares. We talked about books such as *The Friendship of Women* written by Dee Brestin or *Disciplines of the Beautiful Woman* by Anne Ortland. As a busy young mom, I found out that it was so nice to have someone pay attention and care about me. My own mother did not live in the same town, so it was extra special to have Joy in my life.

When I walked into her home, her husband greeted me, and then he generally headed to his woodworking shop, so we had a beautiful, quiet space to enjoy conversation. She was a delightful lady. Her voice sounded like music. She was comforting to be with—I truly loved being in her presence. As it was time to go, she always "walked me out," and we'd extend our good-byes in the driveway. She would always send me off with a hearty wave, and I loved seeing her in my rearview mirror until she was out of sight. To this day, I love walking people out, and I always think of Joy as their car disappears.

I remember the day I found out that Joy was sick. When you hear the word "cancer" it's not easily forgotten. As Joy underwent treatment, she remained positive and uplifting. She continued to be a beacon of light for me and for so many people.

I tried to think of some way to encourage her in the same way she had done for me. So, I had the idea to set a table for her, like she had done for me on many occasions. I packed a picnic basket with two teacups, an assortment of tea, cookies, and napkins and drove to the hospital where she was receiving treatment.

As I was in the elevator on my way to Joy's room, a nurse asked me about the basket. I told her what I planned to do for Joy. She said, "I have never seen anyone bring a tea party to someone here. That is special!"

And it was.

She said, "I have never seen anyone bring a tea party to someone here. That is special!"

Joy and I sat together and talked like we always did. I took some pictures with my camera, but you know what? I also took some pictures with my heart that day. Her face lit up, and she smiled as we sipped our tea and ate our cookies and shared some time together. It created a special memory for each of us.

Joy fought cancer for six years, and during that time, she not only continued to teach me how to live, but she taught me how to die with grace. She displayed kindness and strength, even in her final days. I will always remember our teatime in the hospital. It is a memory I continue to cherish.

Bring dinner during life transitions

I have always believed that a home-cooked meal is a true labor of love. It has been my pleasure to bring meals to people when they are going through big transitions, tough times, or unique circumstances. I think the gift of a lovingly prepared meal can sometimes convey more than words can.

Sometimes, when a friend or a friend's child has a new baby, I like to drop off a meal. A meal is a way of saying, "Just relax tonight. I have this covered for you!" I take the meal along with a card. I write the menu on the card and a note on the other side. I like to make it beautiful enough that someone would be able to keep it in their baby book or as a special momento of this wonderful new time of life. In fact, I recently received a text from my friend, Cece, who was going through her daughter, Anna's, special keepsakes. She sent me a photo of the menu I had made for her years earlier and she still remembered the meal! Along with the meal, I might tuck in some bubble bath cubes and a pretty magazine with a note that the new daddy is in charge while the new mama enjoys some uninterrupted alone time.

A meal is a way of saying, "Just relax tonight. I have this covered for you!"

When I arrive at the home of a new baby, I set up the meal on the kitchen counter with the meal card placed where it can be seen. I am sure to bring disposable containers to the new parents, so they do not have to return anything to me. I might snap a picture of them with the meal and their little one. Taking just a few moments to lay everything out is one way to make life easier. After a few minutes of congratulations, I leave them to have dinner because I know they will soon be sleeping! When I was a new mom, this was the absolute most wonderful thing anyone could do for me!

Sometimes, I also include muffins or breakfast food for the couple with a new baby. Since they are up all night anyway, why not deliver something for breakfast for those early morning feedings?

Dinner deliveries seem to be a universal practice. I have never had anyone turn down a meal. Whether they are going through a death in the family, a birth, renovating their home, or moving into a new place, times of transition can be stressful. By delivering a meal, we give that family an evening without the preparation and hassle of cleaning the kitchen. It is a delivery of rest!

Now that our children are grown, I see that the three of them have caught the vision of helping others. I've seen our son, Michael, share a meal by grilling on his Big Green Egg and hosting friends for dinner. I love seeing how he has had fun opening his home to so many people since he got his place a few years ago. And, he's become quite the chef, too! He'll send photos in our family group text of what's for dinner and I'm totally impressed with what he's serving! I have seen our daughters, Anna and Betsy, prepare home-cooked meals and also send Uber Eats or DoorDash meals to friends. I think anytime you can deliver a meal, in any capacity, it is the work of hospitality.

Send an article

It is not always necessary to cook an entire meal or drive to the hospital to deliver a special surprise. As I look through the local newspaper or a magazine, I especially enjoy sending an article via mail, text, or email to our son-in-laws, Houston and Michael. I like them to know their mother-in-law cares about what they are interested in. I look for articles that I could send to people in my life.

Recently, I saw an article titled, "Lavender and Lace." It brought a smile to my face as I thought of my friend Sara Bajwa, who owns a business with the same name near Lake Alfred, Florida. I cut out the article and mailed it to her. I know at times things can be difficult for shop owners, and I just wanted to send her happy thoughts. Her restaurant and gift shop has brightened my day many times, so why not brighten her day as well? I sent her a note, along with the article, to tell her what her shop has meant to me over the years.

I enjoy looking for articles for my husband as well! I give him articles regularly about business or about a new restaurant opening. We both care deeply about organizations such as First Orlando, Generous Giving, Lift Orlando, NCF (National Christian Foundation), The First Academy, and Victory Cup Initiative. I cut out anything about these entities so he can see exciting new developments. When I find an interesting article for him, it not only shows him that I am thinking of him, but it also sparks new conversation between us. I find that this act of kindness enriches our marriage and our everyday connection.

Hospitality not only changes the relationships outside your home, but it also enriches the relationships with your family.

I have always done the same for our children. For example, our son, Michael, began working in medical sales and leasing in Birmingham after college, so I would find articles about new medical offices in his area and send them his way. I still do that, but sometimes I snap a picture and email it instead. At times, I save relevant articles for him, but whatever method I use to share the article, I know it brings us closer.

Michael now works in the family business, and I love finding articles for him that relate to his work with sales and leasing. It keeps us connected and helps us have deeper and more interesting conversations. I want my husband and family to know that I care about what they do. This is one way to show them. I want them to know that I am interested in what they are interested in, and I am willing to focus on things they love, because I love them.

Friends also appreciate getting an article through the mail. Last week, I sent my friend Kristie an article about how to make hosting a group of friends easier. She texted me a word of thanks and said, "It was so good and useful. I'm taking a picture to send onto our high school friends in Texas. I love that you thought of me. That was so sweet!"

Hospitality not only changes the relationships outside your home, but it also enriches the relationships with your family. Focusing on others is the essence of true hospitality.

Overcome obstacles to make something special

Twelve years ago, I walked to my mailbox and found an answer to prayer. It was an invitation to a Bible Study called Becoming Like Christ. Since I had been asking the Lord what He had for me next, I knew immediately this was the answer. I showed up to the study not even knowing who would be in the group. It turned out that eleven other women were there that day, and we began a journey together.

It was a three-year study that began by us spending the weekend together and sharing our life stories. Each person told the group about her life and journey to that point. We talked about three things: the people, places, and events that made us the people we are today. It was an incredible experience to dig deep that weekend with each other. Our group bonded that weekend, and we have been together ever since! Even when the three-year period was over, we decided to form a little prayer group and continue to support one another. We are fourteen years into our three-year study! It has been a sweet and special group of women who have encouraged me tremendously. We have gone through life events of our children's graduations, college search, going off to school, their first jobs, dating, engagements, bridal showers, weddings, baby showers, our empty-nest experiences, our children's college graduation, and becoming grandmas. We have lost spouses and parents. Through it all, we have been privileged to be a part of each others' lives. We have been through so many stages of life together, and it has truly been a group filled with sweetness. We no longer meet as often as we did, but I know I can count on those women to pray immediately with just a text, no matter where any of us are!

No matter the circumstances, we can go the extra mile to show people that they are special.

When the pandemic brought our world to a halt, it stopped so many events from taking place. However, I have been able to witness a group of ladies who used their imagination and strength to forge ahead with such memorable moments.

We have now hosted a few "Zoom showers" that have infused creativity into our hospitality. We mailed beautifully wrapped gifts to the house of the mom-to-be. We sent her decorations through the mail. One of the new moms honored was our daughter, Anna, and her husband, Houston, who were expecting their first baby in Atlanta. The girls even mailed the same cookies and tea bags to each attendee so we could all enjoy the same thing together at the same time in different cities. Once we gathered using technology, I worried that the event would lose its sweetness, but by the Lord's grace, it did not. I was so glad Anna was with her wonderful mother-in-law, Jan. She wasn't alone at her own baby shower.

Each person in the group shared a story or a bit of heartfelt advice for the new mom. She listened and took it all in. We each shed happy tears as we spent time together, although miles apart. Even though it did not look like a traditional baby shower, it was still filled with the same love.

I was encouraged by the fortitude of the group to make sure that this day was special and that our daughter felt loved, no matter what. Despite the circumstances, we can go the extra mile to show someone that they are special and that their big life moments do not go unnoticed.

Speak to the manager

I think when most people hear the words, "I'd like to speak to the manager," they tend to think a complaint is about to be spoken. I have always believed that words are powerful and nothing is better than encouraging someone who is doing a good job. Appreciation goes a long way!

When our children were young, I had a little red sticker with a teddy bear on it that said, "I caught you being good!" I love emphasizing the positive, instead of focusing on the negative. I guess I just continued looking for the good in people as the years went by. A little happy goes a long way.

Often, if we have had an especially good server at a restaurant, we'll ask to speak to the manager while we are still enjoying our meal, and we'll let the manager know how pleased we are. Many times, as you leave a restaurant, the hostess will ask, "Was everything okay?" This is an open invitation to pass along a compliment. I believe if we look for the good in people, we will find it. The actress, Betty White, at 99 years old, said she was born "a cockeyed optimist. That never changed. I always find the positive." I guess I am like that too, and I credit my own parents, Beverly and Vernon Moline, for that, as well. They have always been some of the most positive and encouraging people you would ever get to meet. Everyone who knows my mom and dad will mention that about them. They love people and are truly interested in encouraging others. People are naturally drawn to them, young and old alike.

If I am on the phone and someone has offered exceptional service, I like to pass a compliment along, too. Call the store manager when you have gotten excellent customer care, rather than just calling when you are upset with their service. More people call and complain than call to praise and compliment. It's easy to complain when something isn't right, and I will if it's appropriate, but I especially look for a chance to pass along a good word. There is so much good in our world if only we look for it.

Appreciation
goes a long way!

1) Did you have tea parties as a child? What do you remember about them?

2) What is one of your favorite meals to cook or eat out? Is it the kind of meal you can share with others?

3) Do you remember a person who showed you great customer service? What did he or she do?

4) What ideas do you have for taking hospitality on the road?

CHAPTER FIVE

Friendship and Openness

*Openness
invites joy*

It is my joy to stay open to knowing someone new, to connecting with a person along my path, and to making a stranger a friend. The essence of hospitality involves an open spirit. Without an open heart, my focus becomes too narrow, only seeing my current friends and the people whom I am expecting to see. By keeping my eyes open to others, whether I am expecting to see them or not, I have the privilege of being a part of serendipity.

We recently took a trip to North Carolina and were privileged to stay at The Greystone Inn. It was recommended to us many years ago, and I tucked it away as an idea for a "special someday." Scott and I love historic hotels! As we walked through the hallways of the inn and gazed upon the black and white pictures of people on the walls, we both felt a sense of connection to those who had been there before us. I love imagining people who have gone before me walking those very same halls. I had so many questions about the hotel, its visitors, and the founders. Luckily, our concierge, Melanie Smith, was willing to share with us about the hotel. She told us stories about when Henry Ford was a guest at the hotel many years ago. How remarkable to learn that notable families, such as the Edisons and Rockefellers, had stayed at this lovely place, too. She made the whole place come alive as she shared her love of this inn. Melanie went above and beyond her normal call of duty by giving us advice about books to read, such as one we now love titled, *Treasures of Toxaway*, which I treasure myself. It was fun to locate the book at a bargain price on eBay and see that it was even signed by the author. After our visit, I felt that it would be important to drop a note to the owner of the hotel and let him or her know that Melanie had enriched our visit with her knowledge and enthusiasm.

> *The essence of hospitality involves an open spirit.*

Melanie and I not only enjoyed conversation, but we began a friendship on that trip. Eighteen years ago, I had cut out an article for a "someday trip" to The Greystone Inn. I loved being able to give the *Southern Living Magazine* article to Melanie to keep in her notebook. I knew she would appreciate it. I have shared more articles with her and returned to talk with her again. Although I didn't plan to make a new friend at the entrance of the hotel, I am thankful for how our connection has enriched my life! A hospitable and welcoming heart makes room for unexpected friends.

On that same trip, as we were checking in, and a young man overheard us mention that we were from Orlando, Florida. This man kindly stopped us and said, "I heard you say that you were here from Orlando. I know there are 2½ million people in that city, but do you happen to know the Boyds?"

Scott and I looked at each other and we smiled and said, "Well . . . we *are* the Boyds!"

It turns out that he played golf on the men's team at Auburn University with our daughter, Betsy, who was on the women's team. He even told us, "I have been to your house. I played Bay Hill with Betsy and your son, Michael, many years ago and stopped by to meet you after our round."

Scott laughed and said, "I probably paid for that round of golf!"

Later that evening, we ended up having a two-and-a-half-hour dinner with Jamie and his wife, Bo. It was such a delightful evening, full of stories and laughter. We heard about how the two of them met in Thailand when he was playing on the Asian Tour. We heard about their lives now. We did not plan it, but in a beautiful moment of providence, we met some new friends right there in a hotel lobby, 600 miles from home.

I believe there are wonderful people in the world, and it is my privilege to connect with them. By staying open to the idea that new friends are right around the corner, life is more exciting. I never know who I might meet next, but I try to be ready when they come into my life. I am ready to make new friends and to invite them into our day. Staying open is a small way to add a spark and richness to your everyday life. Our lives are made up of a million small moments, and I want all of mine to count.

"I would rather have thirty minutes of wonderful than a lifetime of nothing special."

ROBERT HARLING

Robert Harling, author of the screenplay for *Steel Magnolias*, wrote, "I would rather have thirty minutes of wonderful than a lifetime of nothing special." Me, too!

Make time for something new

Other places I love to visit while traveling are the local libraries or independent bookstores. Author Justin Travis Calls writes, "What is it about old books that makes them smell so delicious?"

Often, local libraries have sales on books, and I can keep them myself or give those books to friends and family members as surprises. When we were recently in the library in Blowing Rock, North Carolina, I asked if they had any used books by a favorite author of mine, Jan Karon, since that is close to her hometown. They had several, so I bought them and planned to give them to some of my friends back home and introduce them to her writing. They are delightful stories of small-town living. They are books that have happy endings, kind of like a Hallmark movie, if you know what I mean.

However, later that afternoon, Scott and I went hiking, and we saw a couple who were both working on art. The man was painting while his friend was sitting and sketching. They motioned to us to come closer and see what they were doing. We ended up having a wonderful conversation with them. Scott and the painter, whose name was John, talked and he shared with us about his military service. As we enjoyed the beautiful mountain view, the woman named Lena, and I talked a little bit about Jan Karon and why I loved her books. The woman seemed very interested, and even though my original plan was to give the books to specific friends at home, I decided to go back to our car and surprise her with the books I just purchased. She seemed delighted! She gave me a hug, and we continued to talk. As we tried to walk away, she said, "Can I give you another hug?" She was truly grateful for the books, and I was truly grateful for our time together.

Being sincerely interested in people makes a difference in your own life.

Although Scott and I had simply planned to spend time together walking around the lake at Moses Cone Park that day, I am thankful that he has a similar attitude about inviting new people into our day. As he and I travel through life together, we are enriched by the conversations we have with strangers. Not all conversations turn into friendships, but they make our experiences deeper. We were open to learning about art from new friends on the trail and learning about a hotel from someone who shared the history of that place with us.

We believe that everyone has a story. Being sincerely interested in people makes a difference in your own life. It has opened doors to conversations that we won't forget. Being sincerely interested in people makes your own life richer.

Take a chance and give the invitation

When I was a brand-new mom, still trying to figure it all out, I decided to take an infant CPR class in downtown Orlando. New moms are often juggling a lot, and I was a few minutes late to the class. As it would happen, another young mom named Beth arrived late as well. When we both settled into the class, the teacher paired us with each other, and we had a great time getting to know one another.

As the class ended, I decided to take a chance. My exact words were, "I know this sounds really weird, but would you want to come over for lunch?"

She didn't think it was weird! She came over, and Beth became one of my dearest friends. In fact, I recently sent her a card that read, "Thank you for being late!" We still count on each other to be five minutes late, and I'm so glad we do.

"I know this sounds really weird, but would you want to come over for lunch?"

Although openness does involve some risk and even some courage, it is so worth it! At times we all have to be brave enough to initiate a conversation, make a phone call, or extend an invitation to lunch. Not all invitations end with friendships, but when they do, it makes our lives more meaningful.

Through Beth, I met another dear friend named Terri. She and her husband, Scott, ended up partnering with my Scott and me to teach a newlywed class at our church for many years. If I had not taken the chance to invite Beth to my house, I also may have missed out on meeting Terri. Bravery can have a ripple effect, so when you feel a twinge of fear, don't allow it to prevent you from taking a step of faith and extending hospitality to a person in your path.

In 1980, I had only been married for a couple of months when I found myself downtown at our church. As I went into the ladies room, before the choir practice, I overheard a woman chatting with her friend about the Northwestern Bell Telephone Company. Excitedly, I thought, "*She is probably from my hometown of Minneapolis.*" I didn't want to interrupt her, so I looked under the stall and saw her shoes. Later I found those shoes and introduced myself. That introduction turned into a mentorship that truly changed the course of my life! Joy Torell and I met in a most unlikely places—a ladies bathroom! I was a young newlywed, a long way from home and my own wonderful mother, Beverly Moline. Joy became one of the greatest gifts of my life!

I must tell you another story . . . I met another dear friend, Debbie, in another unexpected place, and this time it was the public library in Longwood, Florida. She was there with her three little girls. Our four-year-old daughters, Emily and Betsy, began pushing little chairs around to "make a train." Debbie's family was new in town from the New Orleans area. We would be moving ourselves within the year to Charleston. As I met her, I knew that would be me in a few short months. I felt compelled to reach out and invite them to our home. The funny thing is, we have been best of friends now for thirty-two years, but have only lived in the same town for less than a year! I guess you'd call that a pretty special long-distance friendship. The wonderful thing is our husbands, Scott and Chris, became good friends as well. Pretty awesome where that little library "train" took us!

I am not suggesting that you hang out in bathrooms or government buildings just looking for people whom you can befriend, but when you come across someone with a common bond, go for it! Take a chance to open your life to someone when you least expect it. In the moment when you could take a leap of faith or stay quiet, I encourage you to choose boldness. Just say, "Hello!"

MAKE THE CONNECTION.

EXTEND THE WELCOME.

START THE CONVERSATION.

*Look for
someone
who needs
a friend*

When my children were young, I attended a Thanksgiving feast with our youngest, Anna, at her preschool, and I saw someone who walked in by herself with her little boy. I simply asked, "Are you alone? Would you like to sit with us?" She thanked me and let me know that she would love to do that. I discovered that her name was Betsy, the same as our daughter's name, and we had so many things in common. I felt as though our hearts were linked right there at that little table with our children. That was almost thirty years ago, and we have been dear friends ever since. Had I never asked her to join us, who knows if we would have begun our friendship?

Simple hospitality can happen anywhere and anytime if you just look for it.

Hospitality has so much to offer. It offers friendship and connection. It offers moments of true heart connection. Although it may begin with bravery and an open heart, it gives so much back that you will never even remember that you took a risk. It can begin with offering kindness to someone who is alone. Betsy's husband, Doug, was working that day and was not able to attend. I never knew all the kindness Betsy would return to me over our many years of friendship.

One of my favorite ways to be hospitable is to look for someone who appears to need a friend. A recent study showed that nearly half of Americans have three or fewer close friends, and that trend has grown considerably in the past few decades. Who is sitting alone? A warm smile and a kind word could make more of an impact than an evening of hosting people in your home. You can be giving someone a gift by inviting them to be your friend.

A crowd is a terrible place to be by yourself.

Simple hospitality can happen anywhere and anytime if you just look for it.

Last summer, my husband and I attended a funeral and discovered that hospitality can make a difference in the most unlikely places.

I noticed a friend, Sandy, walking in alone. I thought that no one should have to sit alone at a funeral. It's difficult enough to grieve, but doing so by yourself would be especially tough. I simply asked, "Are you here alone? Would you like to sit with us?"

"Yes, absolutely," she answered.

A crowd is a terrible place to be by yourself. By looking for people who need a friend, I have made friends in the most unexpected places. I have never regretted reaching out to someone in his or her time of need, whether that meant dropping off a meal or initiating a conversation. The sweet connection that can follow makes life worth it! I've always said, "I don't want to miss my chance."

Tell me
your story

I spent the day with a dear friend of mine, Betsy. We had a beautiful time together as we traveled up to her home in the mountains of North Carolina. We stopped for lunch in a quaint tearoom that had been recommended to us in the small town of Fletcher, NC and got to talking with our server who took care of us. We ended up being the last ones in the tearoom. As we got to know each other better, she opened up about surviving breast cancer. We met many people along our path that day and were able to hear many of their stories. By the end of the day, Betsy said, "I cannot believe all the people we have met today!"

I laughed as I realized I naturally try to get to know people I randomly meet. I try to learn their names and develop a bit of a relationship throughout the course of a normal day. I am particularly drawn to people who are not like me. I love to hear about their journey and their experiences. It is an enriching way to live, as I never know what stories I will hear. Sometimes, it is just a quick hello or a smile, but every now and then, it turns into more than that when you least expect it. I want to live in these moments, in the little spaces along the way of life.

One day, I was taking a computer class at a local store. The young girl helping me had a spectacular tattoo on her arm. I couldn't help but ask her, "Tell me about your tattoo." You'd be surprised how people love to tell you about the special meaning behind their tattoos. I have learned that if someone takes the time to imprint something on his or her body, there is a story that person wants to tell. In fact, we all have some kind of story, don't we?

We all have some kind of story, don't we?

Many people like to talk about themselves and notice when someone is interested. People want to be heard. It is amazing what people will tell you when you ask. I believe many people have something important to say, something to teach, and something to share. I also believe that some people are looking for an invitation to open up about their life. I enjoy giving the invitation and creating a space where connection is possible.

The question, "Tell me about your tattoos" is just one of the phrases that I have used with new people over the years. However, I have heard of so many other ways that help people feel comfortable and accepted. Other simple questions are, "What brings you here?" or a sincere, "How is your day going so far?" Each question is designed to show interest for new acquaintances, and to give insight into their worlds.

When you show interest in someone else's world, you are showing hospitality. I have always believed that hospitality is an attitude as well as an action. The reason I love sharing simple moments is because they are unique to each person. It is a warm welcome to sit down and listen. It is a gentle spirit that is open to hearing. It is taking time for people. It is a willing heart to empathize and connect with people on a deeper level. Sometimes we just have a moment to make an impression on someone, good or bad. I want to make the most of my moments.

1) How did you meet some of your best friends?

2) Can you think of a time when you needed courage to meet someone?

3) On a scale of 1 to 10, how interested are you in the stories of others?

4) When do you remember being new to a place (school, neighborhood, church)? What did it feel like?

5) Share some of your story with this group—the story of your family, your hobbies, or your home.

C
E
L
E
B

CHAPTER SIX

Parties and Gatherings

Get in the party mindset

I love to host a party! It is one of those wonderful joys to invite others into our home. I believe the right mindset about parties and gatherings can make the process of hosting more enjoyable for everyone.

I have always thought of a party as an actual gift that I am giving to each person who is attending. Granted, it is a lot of work to prepare your home, but I love offering that to people. With each gathering you have you are preparing for the coming joy! I like to think that each party we host has a purpose. One of the most important purposes is connecting people. A party is a great place to do that because it should be relaxing and just plain fun! It is a place where they can maybe forget the worries of the world for a short while and feel completely cared for. From the moment they walk in the front door, I want others to feel welcomed and relaxed. It is my goal that each person who attends a gathering of ours feels at home and encouraged throughout the evening. A friend once told me that when she walked into our home, it felt like our home was giving her a "hug." I loved that!

I do like to be organized. When everything is ready before our guests arrive, I am free to give my full attention to welcoming people and enjoying them. When my attitude is relaxed, our guests follow suit. If I am unprepared and stressed, the atmosphere will not be right for those I have invited to our home. So, I begin with organization and the intention for a cozy experience for all, including me! If I have invited someone who I know isn't acquainted with many people, I try to let a few friends know that ahead of time so they can help the new person feel welcome.

When my attitude is relaxed, our guests follow suit.

One year, I hosted a large Christmas cookie exchange for a special group of women. It was a holiday tradition and that year, our daughter, Betsy was five years old and old enough to attend. I wanted her to really enjoy this event as it was one of my favorites. However, a few minutes before the first guest arrived, I heard a crash come from the living room and instinctively knew that our Christmas tree had fallen over. Rather than stress out and become overwhelmed with fixing the tree, I decided to let it go. I was making punch, and resurrecting the Christmas tree was not on my to-do list! I refused to let it ruin my evening with these special women and my precious daughter. That particular year holds a fond memory, believe it or not, of the twenty-five years of Christmas cookie exchanges that I hosted. It was memorable to say the least!

I am so glad I made that decision! It ended up becoming a wonderful memory because as friends came in, it seemed that everyone wanted to help prop up the tree and put on one or two ornaments, and it drew people together who didn't even know each other as they worked together for a few moments. As our children were growing up, we would give them a new Christmas book each year. That year, *Mr. Willowby's Christmas Tree* by Robert Barry was perfect as it told the story of a Christmas tree that was way too big. I put a photo of our "way too big tree" that had fallen over on the inside cover of the book to remind us of that year. When guests are coming to the house, I have found that my mindset and my intention are more important than anything I could prepare for them. I try to begin with a relaxed and joyful attitude. With that end in mind, I am more focused on making my guests feel comfortable than impressing them with anything in our home.

Creative ways to celebrate

Although I love birthday parties and good ole Fourth of July picnics, I have found that a little creativity helps to make the entire event memorable, and it even catalyzes unexpected friendships and conversations.

For example, one of my favorite evenings was when we hosted a Death by Chocolate party right around Valentine's Day. Each person was invited to bring something red, like strawberries, or their favorite chocolate dessert, along with a photo of their wedding. We shared how we met our spouse, and had special conversations about the early days of love and marriage. What a unique night with some incredible laughter through tears! It was one of those nights when your face hurts from laughing so much! It all began with a spark of creativity! It was a huge hit. It set the mood for everyone to share new stories and get to know each other on a deeper level.

For our newlywed class that we taught, we loved hosting a Road Rally. This party involved following clues around town with other couples as we raced to the finish line. By working on a scavenger hunt together, we noticed that couples became friends faster as they forgot about the usual dinner chit chat and dove headfirst into the competition. The evening culminated back at our home where everyone shared their adventures with the group.

Creativity is not just for inviting conversations with adults. Our children hosted some memorable parties that still warm my heart. Our son, Michael, invited his buddies to a golf birthday party where the boys and girls played and had a friendly competition with lunch afterward. Another favorite of mine was the Best Loved Doll Party. Each little girl brought her favorite doll, and we made an afternoon of playing together with them. The attendees not only dressed up, but they also dressed up their dolls.

The circumstances forced creativity, and then it turned out to be a wonderful surprise.

We had a special award for each doll and plenty of punch for everyone. I got the idea from an old book with the same name, by Rebecca Caudill. Our daughter, Betsy, made little awards out of pink construction paper hearts. Our daughter, Anna, loved the character Winnie the Pooh when she was in the first grade. Her party was a special memory, complete with "dirt dessert" in a little clay pot with gummy worms. I think parties at home where you don't have to spend a lot of money are the best.

At times, the circumstances can force creativity, and then it could turn out to be a wonderful surprise. We kept trying to get together with our next-door neighbors, Cor and Lauri, for a dinner party, but we had trouble finding babysitters again and again. One night, we quit trying to make it work and just decided to have Dessert in the Driveway. We put the kids to bed, brought our baby monitors out with us, set up a card table and chairs, and finally connected in a new way. It was wonderful and certainly memorable!

Creativity can come from a myriad of different places, but whenever it's applied, I find the laughter to be a bit louder and the memories stick a bit longer.

Gather people to help in a difficult time

Although parties are generally given to commemorate something happy, I have found that gathering friends can also provide healing. Not long ago, my friend Paula lost her husband, Mike, to cancer. I could not imagine the grief she was feeling.

As Valentine's Day drew near, I kept thinking about her and how it would likely be emotional for my friend to spend this holiday alone. To help her through it, I gathered some of her close friends for a meal. Although the meal was to be at a restaurant, I went over early with name tags and a pretty bouquet of fresh red and white flowers. I wanted to make the table beautiful for her. During the meal, we all shared what we admired about Paula. We spent time letting her know what she means to us and how she has impacted our lives.

After the meal, I invited everyone back to our house for fresh strawberry pie that I had made. I don't think it was the pie we were all craving. It was the treasure of friendships, gathering to support someone who was dealing with a tragedy, that drew us together.

Parties are not the only way to encourage someone when they are worn down. When we have had company stay with us and there is a young mom who is likely tired from chasing children and staying up late into the night, I offer to run a bubble bath. I prepare the room with soft music and candles and bring her a glass of sparkling cider or wine. Then I let her relax and refresh.

I have done this for our daughters when I know they have had a particularly hard week. They don't always have time to be pampered during a regular week, but sometimes they can find the time while our families are on vacation together.

If I can make our home into a soft place for my loved ones to land, then I am offering them the gift of rest.

Making your home a haven for someone who is exhausted, hurting, or just experiencing pain and loss can take many different forms. The point is to put yourself in someone else's shoes. Once you think about what that person may be experiencing, you can create a restorative place to counteract his or her pain. If I can make our home into a soft place for my loved ones to land, then I am offering them the gift of rest.

Invite your child's teacher to dinner

Each year, as we began a new school year, I reminded our little ones, "Why don't we invite your teacher to dinner with our family sometime this year."

When Michael invited his kindergarten teacher, we had coached him on how to treat his special guest. He greeted Miss Scott at the door with a welcoming smile. He invited her into our home and gave her a tour of his room and special toys. He even pulled out her chair for her at dinner. We wanted him to learn how to be a gentleman from a young age.

I still remember his look of pride as he dined with one of the most special people in his life. This was a perfect time to work on his manners and conversation skills, when it mattered most to him. I loved seeing him treat his special guest with such care, and I think the teacher genuinely felt appreciated by the evening with our family.

Often the teacher would read a book with our children, or the teacher and children might swing on the front porch swing together. They had the opportunity to develop a friendship that would make class time even more special.

After we all finished dessert, Michael walked her out to her car and said, "Good night." It truly was a good night for us all! I wanted my children to have a deeper understanding of the people they spent time with every day. It was also nice that the teacher got to know our child, a little bit more of his background, and his family life. Is there a teacher in your child's life that you can invite to dinner?

For Anna, we surprised her on her sixth birthday in an unusual way. It was a Saturday morning, and she had hopped in the car on her way to her basketball game. But instead, we slipped a blindfold on her and told her there was no basketball that day. Instead, we were taking her to an unknown location. We had her put on a "party dress" and arrived at a beautiful tearoom. And who was sitting there to meet her but her kindergarten and first grade teachers, Miss Scott and Miss Faust! It was such a fun memory.

When we invite others to be a part of our world, to go deeper in our friendship, the result is always sweet. You will never regret taking the time to plan an unforgettable evening with your children and the special people in their lives!

When we invite others to be a part of our world, to go deeper in our friendship, the result is always sweet.

When Anna graduated, this same teacher, who had married and become Mrs. Tracie Wood, wrote a beautiful letter of encouragement for Anna's senior book. The teacher has been a special gift to our entire family. What started as a fun morning turned into a lifetime of closeness.

Have you ever thought of writing a letter to one of your favorite teachers? I had the surprise of my fourth grade teacher, Mr. Nelson, "finding me" after nearly thirty years! He and his wife had attended our wedding, but then we had lost touch. His wife, Judy, encouraged him to locate me to let me know they still put up a Christmas ornament I had given him many years ago when I was in his class. They sent a picture of it on their tree, "front and center," as they called it. He wrote me a letter asking if I would mind if he could still call me "Jeffiner," the nickname he had given me when I was in his class. I sat in the car at the top of our driveway, crying my eyes out, reading his letter and thinking back to those innocent days at Garden City Elementary School. Maybe you can locate one of your favorite teachers or better yet, be blessed with the surprise of your teacher locating you!

Anniversaries

Who says you cannot give an anniversary party or surprise to a couple on their special day? We did just that for our friends Ken and Kristie, who were celebrating their 30th anniversary. We told them to prepare for a fun evening, but we gave no details. While traveling in the car, we had questions for them so we could find out how they met, etc. We picked them up and took them to a French restaurant, Le Coq Au Vin, in the heart of Orlando. They loved it, and we enjoyed giving them a beautiful memory!

For our 30th anniversary, we planned to stay at one of our favorite hotels in town. When Scott stepped out of our room, I quickly decorated our room. My mom had saved a white paper mache bell, a decoration from our wedding day, so I used that as a part of the decor for the room. I had even brought along our wedding album so we could look through it and reminisce together. I gathered all the anniversary cards our friends and family members had sent us, and we read them together on that special evening. It is fun to decorate your home away from home, even if it's just for a night or two.

Use the best of what you have for life itself is a special occasion!

We had an unforgettable night, laughing and thinking about our blessings over the years. One of the most remarkable gifts we ever received was a surprise our kids put together for our 40th wedding anniversary. Betsy reached out to almost 100 of our friends and family and secretly put together an incredible book of cards, letters, and pictures for us. It was a priceless gift for her parents. That was such a labor of love as she did that while her two babies napped. Her husband, Michael, helped coordinate with copies of all the responses they received.

Hospitality is not merely for those outside your home. I love to keep Scott guessing by creatively surprising him on days throughout the year. I always say, "Life can be so routine, so why not add some intentional sparkle and savor the surprises along the way?" Maya Angelou said, "This is a wonderful day. I've never seen this one before."

Celebrations are not just reserved for company. They are not to be locked in a closet with the fine china, only to make an appearance during the holidays. Use the china! What are you saving it for? Use the best of what you have for life itself is a special occasion! I love "elevating the everyday!"

Hospitality is a frame of mind, and it is a delight to shower your family with it regularly. This can include a progressive dinner in your own home. We have done that for several Valentine's Day dinners. I have picked up a nice dinner or side dishes at our local Fresh Market grocery store and it's been fun and more personal than being at a restaurant with "the rest of the world" out for dinner on the same night. Why not have appetizers on the porch, dinner in the dining room, and dessert in another room? If it's a busy night and there is no time for something spectacular, I have always been surprised by what simple candlelight can do to make the evening more special.

Whether it is a small surprise or a big one, I think showing people close to you that they are important makes them feel wonderful. It can be an anniversary or just a weeknight. It can be a special date on the calendar or a regular working day. How can you add a little sunshine or a special touch to turn any day into a memory for someone else?

1) Do you enjoy hosting parties? What do you like about it? What do you dislike?

2) What is a creative party you have attended or would like to attend?

3) What gathering would you like to plan next?

4) Who was your favorite teacher as a child? Did he or she ever come to your home for dinner?

CHAPTER SEVEN

Making Intentional Memories

The standout days

When I look back on my days with family, with friends, and even with Scott, I know that some days are more memorable than others. Whenever I spend a little time intentionally creating days that stand out, we all enjoy life so much more! When it comes to hospitality, I believe your family must come first. Today is a good day to have a good day!

We each get one life to live, and we get to choose how to spend it. I believe life is a celebration, and we can celebrate every single day! We don't need to wait for a birthday, anniversary, or a special day on the calendar to do something extraordinary with loved ones.

An example of making a day stand out was when our children were young—we allowed them to "camp out" in our bedroom on the weekend. We did not have to plan anything, we just invited them to bring their pillows and blankets into Mom and Dad's room for "a sleepover" and to have fun together. This began as a special night but turned into a fun tradition! Friday nights became something we all looked forward to. It just kind of happened and became a tradition during a few "growing up years" that we weren't expecting.

When our son Michael was in preschool, the students were learning their colors. When they had Blue Day at school, we all wore blue clothes to dinner that night. When it was Yellow Day in preschool, we ate off yellow paper plates and had a dinner of chicken, yellow rice, and sliced bananas. On Purple Day, we gathered small purple toys from the house and made a purple centerpiece. Then, we ate purple food! We had purple potatoes, purple cabbage, and purple Jell-O, among other things. I realized it's just not all that hard or complicated to "jazz up" dinner or make your kids or family smile.

Those days stand out in my mind. Even without a camera or phone to capture memories, I can see the photos in my mind. When so many school days run together, those do not. Everyone in the family remembers the colorful days.

Today is a good day to have a good day!

Another time, we learned it was National Hamburger Day quite by accident, and we happened to see a cake decorated like a hamburger at our local bakery. We bought the cake and had burgers for dinner. Who even knew there was a National Hamburger Day?

I think my children picked up on the idea of making days memorable. We used any excuse to celebrate. I recall when Anna was a baby and got her first tooth. She was not even one year old, and Betsy was six-and-a-half years old at the time. She looked up at me and said, "Momma, let's put a toothbrush on top of a cake!" We celebrated Anna's first tooth! Pretty simple, huh? Rudyard Kipling said, "Teach us delight in simple things." I have tried to do just that.

When the kids were a little bit older, we all looked forward to the remake of Disney's *101 Dalmatians*. On the day it came out on video, we spread blankets on the family room floor for the kids, and we watched it as a family. That night, we all wore black and white clothes to dinner. Scott did not have a black and white shirt, so the kids secretly took one of his white t-shirts and taped little black construction paper dots all over it! Even the food was black and white. I made roast beef and potatoes, and we ate brownies and vanilla ice cream. Even though our kids were young, they still proudly remember seeing their dad in his white t-shirt with those dots. He was such a good sport! We lovingly refer to it as the Dalmatian Vacation Celebration since it was our first day of spring break.

Can you come up with something fun and memorable to do with the children in your life? Kids don't want stuff . . . they want memories! That's why my husband and I love giving and receiving experiences for gifts these days. My mom has always said regarding gifts that "if she can't eat it or do it..." she doesn't want it! I am now understanding that for myself.

Turn a negative memory into a fun celebration

Have you ever found a lost puppy? Our family found one, and he quickly felt like a member of the family. The kids found him and brought him home with eyes begging, "Can we keep him?"

We hung signs to try to find the owners, and no one responded. We asked neighbors and reached out around town, but we could not find the owner. We finally realized that someone likely dropped the dog off because they could not care for him anymore. We began a search for an adoptive family and found a wonderful one! A local police officer was looking for a second dog, and after meeting with him, the whole family knew this was a great home for our new furry friend.

As the day drew near for the police officer to take the dog, we knew it might be difficult to say goodbye to this special dog the kids had named Snoopy. Even though he was going to a great home, I knew it could be hard to say "goodbye." I decided we would have an adoption party.

It was a time to pause, so why not pause for gratitude? We had enjoyed a lovely time with this puppy, and we took time to celebrate that week together. In every situation, a party is waiting to happen. You are the party planner of your own life! We invited the policeman and his wife and their dog to join our family to celebrate Snoopy's new family. I baked a cake, we put a plastic dog figurine on top, and the simple celebration began.

If your home is not as clean as you would like, dim the lights, light a candle, and enjoy the time you have in your less-than-perfect house. Use the good dishes on a weeknight. Turn a regular, less-than-perfect night into a wonderful memory.

If you can sense that a transition is coming in the lives of your children, your loved ones, or yourself, making the transition positive can have lasting results!

Dim the lights, light a candle, and enjoy the time you have in your less-than-perfect house. Use the good dishes on a weeknight. Turn a regular, less-than-perfect night into a wonderful memory.

*Celebrate
the beginning
and the ending*

When our family dog, Abbie, turned one year old, we hosted a little party. Not only did we invite the neighbors, but we also invited our vet, Dr. Callahan, who is also a family friend, along with his wife and children. The kids loved it! We gave dog bones with big red velvet bows as favors so the neighborhood children could take a treat home to their own dogs.

I think the reason our little sheltie meant so much to the whole neighborhood was because our children worked for two summers to buy her. We told them that they needed to raise half of the money for the family dog, so they worked hard. They had a lemonade stand with a sign (unbeknownst to me!) that read, "Help Us Buy Our Dog." Of course, the neighbors purchased lemonade! We went to the library and chose books about dogs. The kids read books about which dogs were best for children. They interviewed a veterinarian to find out what breeds he recommended. So, Abbie was a part of our whole community!

On the day she arrived at our home, the kids decorated her crate with a large bow made of toilet paper. We played with her throughout the day, and after a full day of activity, she slowly looked up at each one of us one by one and then plopped her head down to sleep. It was a memory we all treasure.

After fourteen years of including her in our life, Scott and I sensed that her time was ending. The whole family took one night to gather around her and tell stories about her. We sat on the floor in our living room, stroking her

Whether you are saying goodbye to a pet, a job, or a home, these special celebrations can be like bookends to mark journeys in the life of you or your family.

back and passing pictures around remembering, as many good times as we could. Everyone laughed and cried for a couple of hours. We celebrated her life together with our family. Then, in a moment that only the Lord could plan, Abbie looked at each one of us and laid her head to rest. That was the final night of her life, and we were all with her.

Since our vet had been with us at the beginning of Abbie's life, I thought it was only fitting that we thank him in the end. I had found a beautiful book in a gift shop about saying goodbye to your dog. I remember reading it and crying for weeks after Abbie passed away. That book, *Going Home* by Jon Katz, truly helped me to grieve. I took the book to Dr. Callahan and told him that it had really helped me, and I thought it might help his clients when they said goodbye to their family pets. The other thing that was helpful to me was writing some memories of our time with her. It was as if I just had to write, write, write. I did not want to forget her. After about three weeks, that persistent feeling to record thoughts was gone. I am happy we now have a journal to remember and honor her life.

One year after Abbie's death, I took a plate of cookies to Dr. Callahan's office and thanked the staff for the extraordinary care they had given our dog. It was a lovely time of closure, and it let everyone in the office know that we appreciated them.

Celebration, gratitude, is not just for the beginning. It can be just as important in the end. Whether you are saying goodbye to a pet, a job, or a home, these special celebrations can be like bookends to mark journeys in the lives of your family or yourself.

The banana bread day

On a recent trip to our local grocery, I noticed a sale. Apparently, banana bread is on special there at two loaves for $5.00 every Wednesday. I thought, *I can use some more spontaneity in my life*. So, I bought four loaves and had no idea whom I would give them to that day, but that is where the fun began.

I drove home to find a silver truck parked in the driveway. Bob was there, helping us with a little bit of landscaping. I knew he had recently suffered a loss, so I wrote a sympathy card and without saying a word, left the note with a loaf of banana bread on his truck.

Next, I saw that two men were picking up supplies from a fire pit they had built for us. I just imagined all the wonderful conversations that we would have around that fire pit. I could just see the memories in the making! I took two loaves to the men and told them I was so thankful for what they had done for us. They were so excited to take home a surprise loaf of bread. They stopped and told me how much it meant to them that I would share my gratitude with them.

Three loaves of banana bread had already been given away in an unexpected, sweet celebration! Finally, I gave the last loaf to a dear man who had recently started working with my husband. We had a wonderful conversation as he stopped to tell me what a blessing it was to work with Scott. I loved hearing the stories about my husband and this man's admiration of him.

My first banana bread day was a success! It was not difficult nor did it involve a lot of planning. It was a day to celebrate people, but I just didn't know who I would be celebrating. If you buy the bread, you will find someone to celebrate!

If you buy the bread, you will find someone to celebrate!

Intentional sporty memories

Another simple way to make evenings stand out is to notice what is happening with local sporting events, and celebrate them within your family. Years ago, when the Orlando Magic basketball team made the playoffs, we all became big fans. We bought a Magic flag, found some blue and black paper plates, and our young children made signs. Even though we weren't going to the game, we hung the signs in the living room and made a night of it! With the Orlando Magic still a new team in the Eastern Conference and since it was their first year making the playoffs, all of Orlando was talking about it. Excitement filled the city! Why not celebrate it at home and bring that energy into the house? When anyone talks about that season, we recall it because we joined the fun from our home.

Sports have always been a great way to make memories with friends and family members. I will never forget inviting our family to watch our daughter, Betsy, as she was presented with an SEC Championship ring in golf at Auburn University. The team went down on the football field in front of a sold-out stadium of 87,000 fans, and the team was announced to the roar of a cheering crowd. We were all there! We invited her four grandparents to celebrate with her. I believe big moments are more meaningful when you can invite the grandparents to be a part of it. Another easy way to make a memory better is to invite special members of the family or friends to commemorate the occasion.

Whether you have colored plates, flags, or special guests, use your own special flair for making each day unique. Life goes by quickly, and you will be glad you took the time to savor those days even more!

Sports have always been a great way to make memories with friends and family members.

1) What days from your childhood stand out in your mind? Why do they stand out?

2) Is anyone in your life celebrating a big milestone soon?

3) Can you think of something, like banana bread, that you would feel comfortable giving to someone in your life this week?

4) What sports teams do you cheer for? Do you gather with friends for those events?

_____

_____

_____

_____

_____

_____

_____

_____

_____

_____

_____

_____

_____

_____

_____

_____

_____

_____

_____

_____

_____

You're invited

CHAPTER EIGHT

Creative Parties

Make friendly connections

I love making connections for people. A party is truly a gift from you to your friends—it's a chance to show them you love them en masse! Life can always use a little spicing up, so give a party! It is a joy to introduce friends to one another and have the chance to start new relationships among people I know. I try to think through what new friendships could form from the gathering.

One of my favorite places to make new connections was at my Back-to-School Brunch for moms. One year, after school began, I invited some moms from my children's school to a brunch that took place early in the school year, when everyone was just forming those new-year friendships.

I try to decorate using things in my home, so for this event, I would put a red wagon full of cheerful teddy bears at the front door. I used a little plastic yellow school bus along with school supplies as a table centerpiece. I kept everything simple so we could all just enjoy being together. The moms dropped off their children at school and came on over! I asked each person to bring five simple, weeknight recipes to share with the group. This would give us new ideas for easy meals to fix during the school year and would kick off the conversation.

To help new guests feel welcome when I have a party, I try to make sure that all the guests introduce themselves. There is something so important about asking and using someone's name. This part of the brunch often brings out a little information that connects people when they realize that they both have a child who is new in school or who loves football or who has lived in Colorado, etc.

Parties are not just events on the calendar when people will show up at your home! They are opportunities to begin friendships and to enrich the lives of those in your circle and beyond.

Parties are not just events on the calendar when people will show up at your home! They are opportunities to begin friendships and to enrich the lives of those in your circle and beyond.

Host a gratitude party

Ten years ago, I noticed some pain in my ankle that continued to get worse over time. I hoped it was nothing. After several consultations with a few doctors, including those at the Mayo Clinic, I learned that I needed full ankle reconstruction. As I learned about the long fourteen-week recovery period, I envisioned months of watching television and reading books and magazines and felt discouraged about the coming months.

A few days before surgery, I asked myself, "How can I make the most of this time?" I made a conscious decision that I would look for the good in the situation. Being positive isn't pretending everything is good. It is choosing to look for the good in everything. I knew I would need to sit and rest a lot, but the doctor never mentioned anything about sitting and watching TV alone. I thought, *I don't want to just get through this. I'm going to try my best to make something good come from it!* So, right then and there, I decided to spend time with people who meant the most to me. I invited about 20 friends to have lunch with me over the next few months. I began to look at it as a true, unexpected gift of time. My in-laws, Bob and Elle Boyd, stayed with us for the first two weeks. What a blessing they were. Elle had been a nurse and knew just what to do. I fell in love with my husband even more as he lovingly cared for me. Our children were attentive, even though they were in college out of state. Our in-town daughter was wonderful and caring.

After the surgery, the special lunches began! My friends showed up with smiles, caring attitudes, and gifts. Most of all, they just showed up! They sat with me and laughed and took my mind off my painful ankle. I took a picture with each friend and family member to commemorate our day, and it truly ended up being a special and sweet time. People went above and beyond to show kindness to me during this time, and I wanted to thank them for their love and support.

Make new friends but keep the old. One is silver and the other gold.

After I made a full recovery, I tried to think of the best way to thank everyone. I decided to have a Thankfulness party, and just called it a Fall Gathering of Friends. I invited each friend who had encouraged me during that time. I decorated the house for fall, which just happens to be my favorite time of the year! I also gave each friend a photo of the two of us and let her know how much she meant to me. That photo was tucked inside a thank you card.

That Fall Gathering was such a hit that I have done that a few more times. Now, it is not just a time to thank my friends for their role in my recovery but a time for us all to stop and show gratitude for friendships, new and old. Maybe you have heard the poem by Joseph Parry, "Make new friends but keep the old. One is silver and the other gold."

If you begin a Thankfulness Party, you never know what might happen! Maybe it will become a tradition. Maybe you will give your friends time for gratitude and for connecting with old and new friends. It can become a full circle of hospitality for you as well!

Know and
be known

One of my favorite sounds on earth is the sound of the doorbell ringing. It means someone has arrived at our home, and the fun is about to begin! Particularly when I have planned an event, the doorbell of the first guest is a special sound. It's time to enjoy all the preparation I have made as I hope to invite guests into a time of being cared for. I have a friend who says, "That sound is terrifying, especially if I'm not ready!" She laughs at the way I love to have a party. Another friend told me, "You can have a party for any reason!" Yes, I admit, I could. I just believe life is for celebrating the small moments, too!

I do love a party, but it's not for the expected reasons. I love parties because they give people a chance to know one another and be known by them. I want my friends to know each other; I just love sharing my friends! Keep your gathering simple and fun. People crave authentic relationships, not perfect lives they can't relate to.

I just love sharing my friends!

I've always thought it would be so fun to have a "Best Friends Party." I'd invite ten people and have each of them bring a best friend. It would be a "Guess Who's Coming to Dinner" kind of night! That's on my list of a someday party!

A party is not just a place to bring people into a room for food. It is an experience. A new question or an interesting activity can open people to new conversations and encourage friends to get to know one another in a new way.

I remember when I was brand new in town, and I was trying to get to know people. I was so tired of having to introduce myself time after time. I would have loved for someone to invite me to have a conversation with people so that friendships could blossom. The whole reason I hosted my first Christmas cookie exchange as a new bride of just six months was to have a few conversations with the only seven people I knew in Orlando. I invited those friends to our little townhouse and asked each person to make their favorite cookie to share. Our home was humble, but I shared what we had. We all enjoyed conversations about the cookies, family traditions, and so much more! I was hooked! I hosted a cookie exchange for the next twenty-five years in a row! Each time, I made a point to invite someone who was new to town. I noticed that there was something about trying cookies, sharing recipes, and the holiday spirit that made it easy for new friends to feel known and welcome.

I laugh at the many cookie exchanges that have grown from those humble beginnings. My sister, Jeana, who lives in Stevens Point, Wisconsin, began her own cookie exchange tradition as well. Jeana is well known in her neighborhood as the "queen of hospitality" as she loves organizing get togethers year-round for the children and their parents. For a brief stint, we lived in Charleston, South Carolina. My friend, Molly, asked, "Jen, who's going to host the cookie exchange?" I smiled and said, "You are!" She went on to do that for many, many years. We have had a Mother-Daughter Cookie Exchange, Newlywed Couples Cookie Exchanges, and more.

I discovered that it was not really about the cookies! It was about an experience for my guests that fostered friendship. They looked forward to being together each year, too. It is a time where relationships can be born or where they can grow. It is my honor to be a part of that process.

Think
about it

Speaking of the cookie exchange, it has changed and grown over the years. Some years, I asked each guest to bring their recipe to share. When our girls turned five years old, I told Betsy and Anna that they were officially old enough to attend the party, *and* they could invite their teacher. As Michael grew and wanted to participate, we made it a tradition that Scott would take him during the party, to see Santa or do something "Christmassy." When they returned home, Michael and Scott would walk each person to her car, holding the door, and helping her carry the basket of cookies. This gave Michael a chance to practice his conversation skills and to show his gentlemanly manners. The women looked forward to that.

One reason why the party changes a little each year is that I think about the party over the next few days to try to decide what parts to keep and what to change. I spend a few minutes thinking about the food, the flow, and even the finale! Generally, if I liked it, I have found that others do as well. Author Christina Lynch said, "One should have things all set and then 'arrive' at her own party to experience it as a guest would." I try to create a party that I would like to attend.

But I also check with a few of my guests by giving them a call afterwards. I ask them, "Who were you able to connect with?" This tells me if I created the mood I was hoping for! Plus, it extends the joy of the party. Another thing that extends the joy is when I tell the moms that it's fun for their kids to "get cookies for breakfast," the next morning. Children always LOVE that!

I try to create a party that I would like to attend.

Receive with gratitude

I must admit that my friends and family have graciously thrown me some thoughtful parties, but I have also been the recipient of kindness in so many forms. One of life's great joys is to receive from others with deep gratitude.

Scott and I have a favorite restaurant in Orlando where we like to spend special occasions. We don't go there often, but we do make a reservation for moments like celebrating anniversaries. So, on our 42nd wedding anniversary, we dressed up for a special evening in our special restaurant, Eddie V's.

When we arrived, our server was smiling with anticipation as she led us to the table.

There is beauty in the giving and beauty in the receiving.

"Happy anniversary, Mr. and Mrs. Boyd," she beamed as she stopped in front of our table.

I gasped! The table was decorated from top to bottom. She had taken the time to cover it with rose petals and flowers. There were table accents from a local shop that read, "Love." We learned our server's name was "Mimi."

We both smiled and felt overwhelmed with gratitude. As we moved closer, we noticed a sign that read, "Scott and Jennifer." As we looked more closely, we saw that it also said:

42 Years
504 Months
15,330 Days

Wow! What a thoughtful thing this server had done to make our night special. We could not believe she had taken the time to create a stellar evening for us. This was way beyond the scope of a job. She had done this out of love and genuine creativity. We wondered if our kids had called ahead to let them know we've always celebrated each month of our wedding anniversary!

We received this gift with open hearts and truly appreciated the whole night. We sat for hours reminiscing about our many years, months, and days together. We basked in the glow of the night and allowed the beauty of the moment to fill our hearts.

As someone who regularly hosts and plans special surprises, I know what I desire for my friends when I plan a special evening. I want them to thoroughly enjoy it. It is one of my greatest joys to provide respite, a moment when they can forget their troubles and feel taken care of. So, when someone does the same for me, I make it a point to receive the gift fully. There are two sides to hosting and two sides to giving. There is beauty in the giving and beauty in the receiving. Both sides are important! Just as we graciously give, we can bless someone by graciously receiving!

1) What groups of people should you introduce to each other?

2) What are you feeling grateful for lately?

3) Jennifer writes, "I like to throw a party that I would want to attend." What kind of party would YOU like to attend?

4) Is it easy for you to receive? Why or why not?

CHAPTER NINE

Traditions and Memories

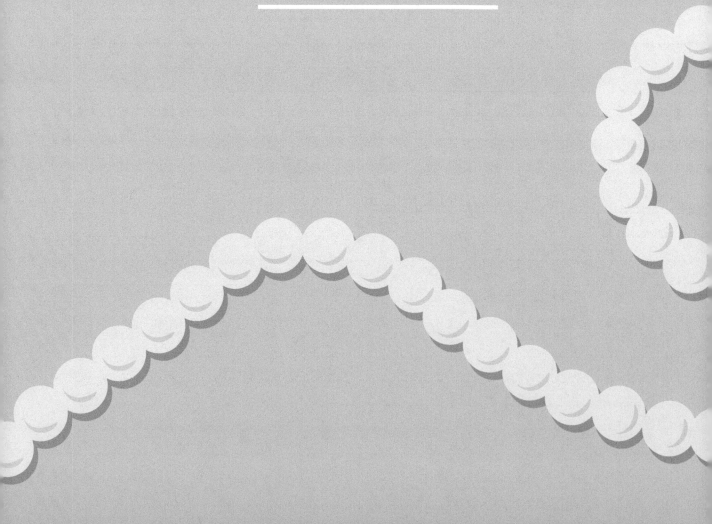

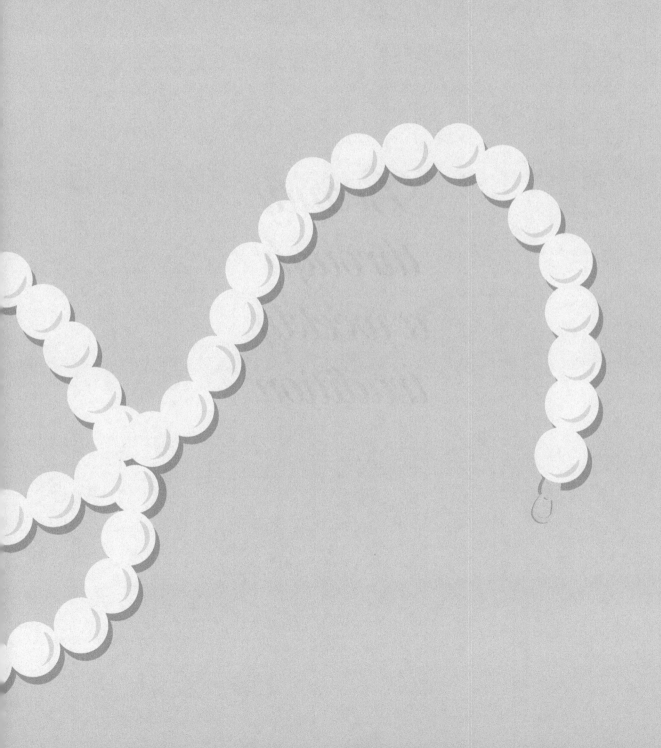

Beauty through a weekly tradition

Saturday has always been a special day for our family. From the early days of our marriage, Scott and I have enjoyed breakfast on Saturdays together. Often, we met our friends Jim and Molly for breakfast at Winter Park's Park Avenue East India Restaurant for a relaxed time of talking and laughing together each week. As newlyweds, we looked forward to this because we were all working, and we rarely had time to just sit and connect. Although the restaurant is long gone, the memories are not.

Although the restaurant is long gone, the memories are not.

This tradition of Saturday breakfast ebbed and flowed as our life changed. There was a long time when our three children were young, and it was just too much work to take them to a restaurant. It wasn't fun. Then, when our oldest, Betsy, began driving, we often took her little Jetta and filled it with gas and surprised her with a car wash on our way home from breakfast. We'd come home, and our three teenagers were all still sleeping in. We hadn't missed a thing.

Now that our children are grown and gone, we have more time, so Scott and I might bring a book or the newspaper to a nearby hotel. After breakfast, we can spend hours in the lobby, reading, writing, and sipping our coffee. It is a time I always treasure because we might be doing various things, but we are together, taking time to discuss the book or article we read, and just enjoying a slow morning.

Now, we often go to Bay Hill or meet friends at the Briar Patch on Park Avenue in Winter Park on Saturday mornings. It's our treat. It's time for a little more relaxed living. Even years ago, when we visited Scott's parents in Naples, we took time for Saturday breakfast with our children and their grandparents at The Cove Inn. Our kids still have great memories of years and years of their delicious, thin pancakes or sitting at the counter watching the cooks prepare breakfast.

Create a beautiful pattern that can see you through more than one decade.

Your special time of the week does not have to be on Saturday. Maybe your family would prefer to enjoy pizza every Sunday night or watch a movie on Friday night. The goal is to create a rhythm that everyone enjoys. Be flexible with how it may change over the years. You are making memories. Create a beautiful pattern that can see you through more than one decade.

*Beauty
in a
holiday
tradition*

If I close my eyes, I can see my mom and dad's little Christmas tree. For 68 years, my parents have had a bubble tree, a special type of old-fashioned tree that is rarely manufactured anymore. They had it the first year they were married back in 1954, and they still put it up now, all these years later! When mom found a local store that sold bubble trees in 2002, she bought one for each of her children. The company had brought the tree back for the 50th anniversary. Now, we all have one in our homes, including my brother, John, who lives in France. Mom and Dad's tree is 68 years old, and would you believe it, it still works!

You can make anything special by declaring it to be so!

When I recently opened the cardboard lid to the box of my parent's bubble tree, I saw Mom's treasured notes. She had briefly written about some of our Minnesota Christmases on the lid of that box. She wrote the date, who celebrated with them, and even a little bit about the weather and the festivities! One said, "Blustery, snowy day with 20-below windchill!" I had never known she had done this. I have been so blessed to be her daughter. I was so moved by her notes that I copied them all to a book for her and Dad as a special gift. It is my joy to share the story of the bubble tree with our own children and grandchildren, so they can look at it and know the history of what it has meant to our family. I have written my own notes and tucked them inside our tree. My mom and I are kindred spirits. My friend Tina says I am intensely sentimental, and I guess . . . I agree! If you have a special tradition or holiday item, share the story regularly. Bring in other family members so you can share it with the extended family. You can make anything special by declaring it to be so! Bob Dylan said, "Take care of all your memories, for you cannot relive them." That's so true!

"Take care of all your memories, for you cannot relive them."

BOB DYLAN

A mom holds so much in her heart. So does a dad and grandparents and aunts and uncles. Write it down. Continue traditions through your written words, whether that is in a book or on the lid of your Christmas tree box.

Share the stories of your holiday traditions

While I was growing up in Minnesota, during winters we had special traditions, different from those we share now in Florida. Each winter, my dad would flood the backyard with water from the hose and freeze it for the neighborhood children to enjoy as a skating rink. He donned his big army coat and thick, warm gloves as he sprayed the hose over our yard day after day, and each of his five children, Jennifer, Jim, John, Joel, and Jeana, sat at the windows, asking the question, "Is it ready yet?"

Finally, after flooding the yard for several days in a row, he would announce, "It's ready!" Our winter ice-skating rink in our backyard was ready to become a winter wonderland. Not only was it a playground for us, but also all the neighborhood children raced to our house for ice skating together. This is one of my favorite childhood memories. My mom would fix Carnation instant cocoa for the skaters as we came into the house to warm up. Dad worked for the Carnation milk company for 37 years, and we all loved that cocoa!

I don't think my parents ever knew what they did for us. They were too busy doing the things that needed to be done with a family of seven. The five of us were "stairsteps" of sorts. We were all born within seven years of each other. I have the "happy gene," a true gift passed on to me from my parents. We learned to find joy in everyday things, like ice skating with all the neighbor kids on 64th Avenue North.

When I saw the Department 56 company created a village piece for their small ceramic Christmas village that was called *Skating Pond*, tears came to my eyes. It reminded me of the years I had spent as a child, skating on the pond my dad created each winter. What a special gift for our family to receive from my parents! When I put it out each year for Christmas, I would tell our children about my early days in Minnesota, about their grandfather, whom they fondly call "Pa," and his big army jacket, and about the neighborhood children skating in our yard all winter. I have written that story down, too, and placed it inside the box. I realize that so many things in our home have stories that are only written in my heart, and if I don't write them down, they will be lost.

"Preserve your memories, keep them well, what you forget you can never retell." ~ Louisa May Alcott

What family stories and memories are important to you? Can you create a tradition, a rhythm, for telling and retelling them so that they continue to bring joy to the next generation?

Our family stories are important to me. What family stories and memories are important to you? Can you create a tradition, a rhythm, for telling and retelling them so that they continue to bring joy to the next generation?

Scott and I spent our wedding night at the Lowell Inn in Stillwater, Minnesota. It is a historic inn that is often written about in magazines. One day, while shopping, I noticed that the Department 56 company had created a Lowell Inn figurine. Not only did I buy one for me, but I bought one for my brother, Joel, who lived in Stillwater, so we can all remember this unique place. I try to teach my children to surround themselves with special things in their home, things that are an expression of what they love and what their extended family loves. If I share these stories with our children and give them items that are special to our family, it brings additional meaning to things. It makes everything more special. It's great that memories written down can be passed from other generations. Can you think of something special you have that has a story that needs to be told?

"Preserve your memories, keep them well, what you forget you can never retell."

LOUISA MAY ALCOTT

174

The beauty of a new tradition

I have always loved calendars, especially the ones from the Rifle Paper Company in Winter Park, Florida. I like to plan my weeks and months, filling them with special times with friends and family members. Buying beautiful calendars has always been a joy at the turn of the year, and I often give lovely calendars to others who share my passion.

I decided to switch it up a little and rather than write my plans on the calendar, I started jotting down what we actually did that day each evening before bedtime. I wrote about conversations, meals, notes sent, and little reminders of beauty that I'd witnessed each day. If life is worth living, it is worth writing about. I try to use time in a productive way. I make a few phone calls to people I haven't talked to for a while. I try and send cards to friends who might not expect them. I try to look for the good in every day. I try to put down my phone and use that time for something more meaningful.

Writing in my calendar at the end of the day was an unexpectedly lovely new tradition. Plans are fun to make, but the serendipity of life is actually more interesting to record. Serendipity can be the one thing we did not plan or didn't even think to ask for, which is what really makes it special, right? I hope that if you embrace this new personal tradition, it will be an ongoing reminder to you that life is good.

Plans are fun to make, but the serendipity of life is actually more interesting to record.

Record and rewrite to make anything special

I truly have amazing friends. They have encouraged me throughout the process of writing this book. Even now, I can see a text message on my phone from my friend Lynn, who writes, "Jennifer, you have the gift of hospitality along with the joy of writing. I'm proud of you for stepping out, pushing a door open." My friend Van said, "I genuinely cannot wait to dive in and see aspects of your special heart on paper." I feel like my book has been patiently waiting for me for a very long time. We all have stories we carry in our soul. It was time for me to put mine on paper. A favorite author of mine, Jan Karon, says, "If you've been saying for at least 100 years, 'I would love to write a book,' I promise you, now is the time." I decided to go for it!!

To stay encouraged and uplifted throughout the writing of this book, I have often copied these sweet messages in my notebook. By handwriting something slowly and with intention, I can truly savor it. I can slow down and really appreciate what my friends have lovingly sent me. I love this saying by Anais Nin, "We write to taste life twice."

I currently have more than twenty pages of encouragement. Each page, each sentence was sent with love. Why should I only read these messages once? If something was sent with such love, I say, "Why not read it again and again?" A text message can be lost so easily. My friend Lisa told me regarding writing this book, "You have a special gift and it's wonderful you are making time to go after it. Sometimes we say 'one day' and that day never comes." These are ones I want to save. That's the thing with emails and text messages, they can be "lost forever" unless we take time to print or write the special ones down. These words of encouragement have helped me to keep going. I love to write things down because my life has felt like a miracle and I don't want to forget any of it.

We write to taste life twice.

If something is special to you, write it. Rewrite it. Read it. Re-read it. Set a time and read important words during a lull in your day. Long ago, I started saving special cards sent to me. If I'm ever feeling a little blue, I pull out my "Cards of Encouragement" file and it's always a treat to reread those words.

Your life only has so many minutes. Why waste a minute complaining or arguing when it could be spent savoring a message of love? Your traditions await you.

1) What traditions are a part of your life now?

2) What traditions do you remember from your childhood?

3) What traditions would you like to begin?

(cont)   Jan 3

We were some of the
very last ones to leave the
American Cemetary tonight.
We were only able to spend
an hour there, but what a
memorable and moving ex-
perience it was! For some
reason I just never thought I
would have a chance to visit
Normandy. I am so thankful
I could and so glad Scott and I
have our three grown children
along as well. I think it will
cause all of us to want to continue to learn more. As we
were leaving, a French man asked me in such a polite way, "are
you looking for the exit?" A nice way
to let me know that's what we should be doing.

CHAPTER TEN

The Pleasure
of Writing

*Menu and
name tags
for your table*

Before guests arrive, I have a few writing habits that add a spark of love and creativity to any endeavor. I like to write the menu on a decorative piece of paper and display it on the table. You could also write the menu on a chalkboard or even on your favorite stationery.

Displaying the menu not only whets the appetite of your guests, but it also lets them know that you have prepared a delicious meal and are anticipating their arrival. It is a simple act of love to complete your table and show your guests that you have been thinking of them. At the top of the menu, I often write the title of the event or give it a "fun" name, something to tip off the guests as to what we are celebrating.

When Michael and Anna returned from France, where they visited my brother and sister-in-law, John and Chrystel, I simply wrote, "Bonjour!" at the top of the page. If we are celebrating a birthday or anniversary, I write, "Happy Birthday!" or "Happy Anniversary to us!" If the meal is during a cold snap, I might even comment about the weather and write the words, "Thought we should have something cozy . . ." When out of town guests join us, I write, "Welcome" and personalize the top of the page. On the last night before Anna left for Samford University in Birmingham, I wrote, "The Last Supper," and the whole family gathered to send her off to school.

The night our grown children came home from France was such a fun memory!

While they were in college, we gave each of our three children the opportunity to go to Europe with airline miles we had saved, so they could have a wonderful time with their aunt, uncle, and cousins. We knew once they graduated and started working "real" jobs, they would find it difficult to get time away. We truly were thrilled and thankful that they had the chance to go visit a new, faraway place. Scott and I had never gone overseas before but hoped we could someday. I teasingly told our kids, "You are sitting in my seat on the airplane!"

The smallest things can make you feel like something special is about to happen.

While Michael and Anna were gone, I guess we were living vicariously through them, because we had dinner at a beautiful, authentic French restaurant in town. It was wonderful to know they were having such a great time with family.

We wanted to make their homecoming special, so we met them inside the airport with fresh sunflowers, balloons, and one French flag and one American flag. It was great to see them, and we loved hearing all about their adventures. Michael and Anna are just a year apart in school, so it was extra nice that they could travel together and have those memories of that experience.

I decorated my little three-tiered kitchen shelf with lots of French-themed things that I gathered from around our house. I had the menu and welcome sign for them on the kitchen island and had prepared a special French meal for them. I felt fancy making cassoulet for everyone and made sure to write it and display it proudly!

This little extra touch shows your family and guests that you thought of them in advance. I do not write a lot or make this step complicated. The menu might read, "Chicken Pot Pie & Tossed Salad & Warm Bread." Add a "We're Glad You're Here," and that's all you need.

When friends or family join us for a meal, I write their names on name tags to show them that I have spent time thinking of the perfect place for them at the table. I find that people are more at ease when they know exactly where to go. It is a small detail that makes the evening flow smoothly and shows friends that they are cared for. Anything I can do to reduce confusion and infuse warmth into an evening increases the likelihood of a fantastic night. The smallest things can make you feel like something special is about to happen.

After many years of practicing this, my friends know I love name tags and they have given me beautiful name tags as gifts. I have a collection for all seasons now! Show your guests that you have thought of the perfect spot for them.

*From my
kitchen to
yours*

Your handwriting is a treasure to your family. Writing is an act of love, and the best news is . . . it's completely free! I absolutely treasure anything I have with my mother's, father's, or grandmother's penmanship on it. My maternal grandmother's name is Helen Hage, but everyone called her, "Ma." She took the time to write a few recipe cards for me many years ago, and I feel connected to her when I read them. Whether it's her famous Homemade Beef Soup or one of her incredible apple pies, I am just grateful to see it in her handwriting. The passing of recipes is the passing of stories. Now that she is gone, it is especially heartwarming to have something that she herself wrote.

It takes me back to when I would get to spend the night as a little girl and pick apples from the trees in Ma and Pa's backyard. I was greeted after school most days by a mom with a warm cake that she pulled out of the oven or something else homemade. I don't know how she did it, but she did. When I asked her how, she smiled and said, "I didn't have a car!"

One day, I realized that I wanted my children to have some of our favorite family recipes in my handwriting. Betsy had requested that as a gift for her 20th birthday. I gathered recipes from aunts, uncles, grandparents, and myself. I wanted the homes of my children to be filled with nostalgic family scents that infused wonderful memories in their hearts as they cooked! The simple act of recording your family recipes can deepen your relationships now as you pass them down and extend your legacy of love and belonging and good food to the next generation. I believe that when recipes are passed down, it's about much more than the food. It's offering a connection to who we are, where we come from, and the people who helped shape us.

Your handwriting is a treasure to your family. Writing is an act of love, and the best news is... it's completely free!

To make the cookbook extra special, I added photos of our family along with the recipes. I have been collecting photos to include in Anna's recipe book, too. I asked Michael if he would like one someday, to which he smiled and said, "Ahhh . . . I'm okay!" But you know what? He's still getting one!

If this project is daunting, another way to combine your handwriting and good recipes is to simply write in your cookbooks. Write a quick two line note or story in the margins of your cookbooks as they relate to your family. It's important to date it so you can remember when you invited guests to your home. At times, when our children were little, I traced their hand in my cookbook as we cooked together. They are only little for a short time! I can now do that with our five little grandchildren: Connor, Will, Margaret, Davis, and Palmer.

I remember one evening I was cooking with our two-year-old Betsy, and we were making a casserole in a glass dish. As I was stirring it, the glass dish slipped off the counter and splattered all over the kitchen floor. My heart dropped. Betsy must have seen the frustration on my face. I could tell I was about to get upset. I took a deep breath and held her little hand. "Let's pray for Mommy," I told her, "Mommy needs patience, and she needs it now!"

I took a deep breath and realized that this moment was bigger than the mess. It was about modeling patience to my sweet daughter. God answered my prayer. He gave me an extra helping of patience that evening, and everything really was fine.

When you turn to the page in my cookbook that reads, Chicken and Broccoli Casserole, you will find the quick story of Betsy praying for my patience. With food and glass splattered all over the floor, and her small eyes looking up at me for my reaction, I knew in my heart what really mattered. It took five minutes to clean up that mess, but it would take much longer to clean up a broken spirit of a child. It was a good reminder for me that children's hearts are tender. I most likely would have forgotten that, had I not written it down.

Meals are not just about ingredients, prep time, boiling, and baking. Meals are full of life! Why not record the beauty of your meals? So much of living takes place in the margins of our lives. Write stories in your favorite cookbooks, even the seemingly ordinary ones about regular moments with your friends, family, and loved ones. Every time I make a recipe, it's fun to see my handwritten notes of special moments we have shared over that recipe, and it always makes me smile.

Write important advice to share with loved ones

My dear friend Darcy describes me as her mentor. Although we did not use that word when our relationship began, it has been a joy to share my heart with her for many years. Even though we live in two different states, Texas and Florida, we have corresponded by phone, written letters, and sometimes, we text. We met when she and Tim had been married just two years, when they were in our newlywed class at church. They moved after just one year here in Orlando, but our friendship continued, and they just celebrated their 30-year anniversary.

Last year, their daughter, Hannah, came to visit. Honestly, when I agreed to host her for an evening, I was worried we would have nothing in common. We had never met, but of course I had heard all about her through the years. She knocked on the door, and I nervously walked to meet her. I could not think of a single topic as I opened the door. But when we saw one another, it only took one smile, a hug, and an invitation. She came in, and we easily talked for the next couple of hours without stopping! We had no trouble finding topics of conversation.

At some point in the evening, Hannah said, "Mrs. Jennifer, what do you think makes a good marriage?"

I thought for a few moments and responded, "Let's wait until Scott comes home, and we can both share our ideas with you."

Scott and I had such a fun evening sharing our thoughts with Hannah! We gave her the honest lessons that we have learned in our 40-plus years of time as husband and wife and raising a family.

It has always been a joy to sit down with young people and share our insights about married life. Whether through a formal Prep for Marriage class at church, an evening with our friends' children, or with someone we may randomly sit next to on an airplane, if asked, it's always been a treat to talk with young people who desire to have a strong marriage.

Before Betsy got engaged, I knew I wanted to spend more than just one evening of sharing advice. I was so thrilled that she would be starting her new life with a wonderful man named Michael Quinn, but I wanted to make sure to pass down the advice that had made a difference in my own life.

I spent time writing, "Advice from a Mom on Marriage"—several pages with thoughts specifically for our daughter. It wasn't a list of dos and don'ts, but rather just a few things to consider before she made that all important life decision. I invited Betsy to dinner and asked her if I could read my notes out loud to her. I have found that asking people permission to give advice is best. It just makes them more receptive. I have had a chance to do that with our Anna as she prepared to marry her wonderful husband, Houston Hough.

Betsy and Anna were both incredibly receptive to my advice on marriage. We had a beautiful dinner as we looked ahead to her married life and thought about marriage together. It is a day I will never forget! I absolutely loved it when she told me later that she thought enough about it to share my thoughts with some of her single girlfriends the next night. If you take the time to write down important advice for important people in your life, I hope it will be a memorable day for you as you pass along your hard-earned wisdom.

I love to listen and try to gain wisdom from people I trust and admire.

When I attended the bridal showers for both of my girls, the older women in the room gave thoughtful advice about how to enjoy married life on a three-by-five notecard. I realized very quickly that I could not contain my advice on a small card. So, I endeavored to write my advice for my children on a few sheets of paper, instead.

Along with giving advice, I have always wanted to receive words of wisdom from people who know and love me. When our children were young, after my parents came to stay with us, I would often ask my own mother if she had any suggestions for me. After all, she and my dad had raised five of their own children, and I knew they had our best interest at heart. I love to listen and try to gain wisdom from people I trust and admire. The Bible even talks about the value of receiving wisdom and counsel from others. I want to learn; I want to always continue to grow.

Fill your Bible with life

Often attributed to Charles Spurgeon, "A Bible that is falling apart usually belongs to someone whose life isn't." Well, what happens to a person whose Bible is full of stories and memories? I can tell you. It's a joy to open the Word each day! I love to read Scripture, but I also like to remember when I read those same words years earlier and what they meant to me then.

When I turn to Proverbs 12:15 (NIV), I read the following: "The way of a fool seems right to him, but a wise man listens to advice."

AUGUST 13, 2008

Anna (17 yrs) goes off to school today. Her 1st day of senior year of high school. Our last "First Day of School" pictures. We've done this for 19 years. End of an era!

When I turn to Proverbs 16:24 (NIV), I read, "Pleasant words are a honeycomb, sweet to the soul and healing to the bones." But I also see the following in my own handwriting: *"Celebrating Mother's Day today, we have all three of our children home. Going to church this morning and then out to The Grand Floridian Café for lunch. A tradition for us for many years."*

And when I open my Bible to enjoy the words of Proverbs 17:6 (NIV), which tells us, "Children's children are a crown to the aged, and parents are the pride of their children," I also delight in my own words, which read:

So . . . I guess we are now the AGED! We have 3 littles with another one on the way. It's a wonderful time of life to have grandchildren! Connor 3 ½ years, Will 1 ½ years, Margaret 4 months.

JUNE 2020

Our kids surprised us with the gift of all gifts, a 40th anniversary book of cards and letters from family and friends. There are close to 80 greetings! What a keepsake and treasure. Also, we woke up to a huge, beautiful sign in the yard, announcing to the world that we are celebrating our 40th.

As I read, Proverbs 21:13 "If one shuts his ears to the cry of the poor, he too will cry out and not be answered." I am reminded that the Bible talks of the poor, they are close to God's heart. Next to that verse, I see my words from 2013:

OCTOBER 2, 2013

Scott is in New Orleans with his friend, Bishop Allen Wiggins, at a conference on being able to work effectively with the poor. (Purpose Built Communities)

One of my favorite verses is Proverbs 25:11 (NIV), which reads, "A word fitly spoken is like apples of gold in settings of silver." It is the right word spoken in the right circumstance. It reminds me of my delightful *Apples of Gold Bible Study*. Beside that verse in my Bible, I see this happy memory:

I have "Apples of Gold" this afternoon at Carrie Gill's house. I love being a mentor in this maturity program for young women.

One final way to add life to your Bible is to ask loved ones to write in your Bible. My 94-year-old father reads his Bible each morning, so during one visit, I asked him to use my Bible and to write in it. He and mom were in town for a few weeks during a winter trip, and he read my Bible each morning. First, it is so wonderful to see him sitting in our family room in the quiet of the morning with the light on reading my Bible. But, he wrote a special note to me in various places in my Bible. I told him not to tell me where he wrote them, so I would come across it and enjoy a surprise! Each time I read his words, I am overjoyed.

Carve out time to write together

Life gets busy, and we have a lot to do, and it's easy to put off important things like writing some of your family history or sharing your story with those you love most. It's even more difficult to make time for you and your spouse to write together.

But that is just what Scott and I did. And I am so glad we made time for it!

Scott has never been a writer. He left that to me! But lately, he has been especially interested in journaling and sharing our story with our children. So, we recently took a trip to Sea Island and stayed in a little cottage along the coast of Georgia to spend what turned out to be a rainy weekend writing our family history for our children and grandchildren. We wanted to put some important names, dates, and thoughts on paper together.

A few questions that guided our discussion included:

- What are some of your favorite family memories?
- What do you appreciate most about each other?
- What words would you use to describe the principles and values that are important to your family?
- What would you like your family to focus on in the future?
- What would we like our family to be known for in fifty years?

Even though our children and grandchildren have heard many of the "family stories," we realized that they have not heard them all in order and not all at once. So, once the writing exercise was complete, we invited the whole family to take part in a special family weekend in town. It emphasized what we already knew; that it's NOT all about us.

Although we entered the time with the idea of writing to pass down the family history, we each enjoyed every minute of it! We relished the memories together as we chatted, wrote, laughed and remembered the times that made our family "us." There are just so many things we don't want to forget, and writing seems to be the only way to keep the joy on the forefront of our minds.

Now, after reliving the shared memories through writing, we have the privilege of remembering everything as we read and share it with our family. Scott and I invited the whole family to take part in a special weekend at a local hotel. We shared memories from our past and hopes for our future.

We feel grateful not only for our family and friends but also for Scott's business, Boyd Development Corporation, which has been part of our lives for over thirty years. He has been blessed with an incredible business partner, Ken Kupp, and team members that feel like family, to share the vision with.

We are so proud to have our son, Michael, working in the family business. He is an intricate part of the day-to-day operations, and yet, he still doesn't know all the stories. We want to share with him and the others the background, the full history, and the moments that made the business what it is today. When we took time to engage in this way, I walked away and thought, "I feel like our family really knows each other in a new way." I felt like it was the most meaningful thing our family had ever done, aside from our family weddings. That's significant. It brought new meaning to our family. We all recognize, it's not about us.

This is the joy of writing! Not only does it give you time to slow down and reflect, but it also allows you to relive the happiness.

Our whole family spent the evening on Friday and most of the day on Saturday together. Not often do you get to have the whole family in a room to discuss your heart. I had written our history so they had something to keep. Scott shared the history of the business and specific challenges and specific lessons learned throughout the journey. It was just a great conversation that began with meaningful writing.

This is the joy of writing! Not only does it give you time to slow down and reflect, but it also allows you to relive the happiness. Why should an event only provide joy once? When you write and read it again and again, you can get even more joy out of a single moment! The time of reflection also provided us with a clearer purpose for the future. When we write things down, we give them value. Writing gives clarity. Sharing your writing with others multiplies the knowledge and joy.

1) Do you enjoy writing? Why or why not?

2) Do you have anything written by the hand of someone who is not with us anymore? Who is it and why is it meaningful to you?

3) What recipe do you think your loved ones would like to have in your handwriting?

CHAPTER ELEVEN

Sweetness

Master a dessert

Life is sweet. I feel that every single day has an opportunity for something delicious. Whether it is a warm conversation or warm chocolate chip cookies, or preferably both, I love to create moments that are truly sweet. Mealtime is a chance to show people that you want to honor them with your time, to make it special for them. With just a little bit of extra effort, any meal can turn into a memory. Any meal can be sprinkled with sugar! Julia Child said, "I think careful cooking is love, don't you?"

Making my chocolate cake now reminds me of celebrations and vacations we have had in the past. Each bite is full of memories. My first chocolate cake wasn't perfect. But I made it again and again, and now, I have complete confidence in it! My advice to young people is to master a favorite meal and master a dessert. I have been making this same cake since our first years of marriage.

If your first attempt isn't a success, try it again. If you taste something you love, don't be afraid to ask someone to teach you how to make it. It was a joy teaching Anna's friend, Katie, how to make my chocolate cake. I felt like I was passing on a culinary tradition to another family and another group of people that would share the same delight. She recently sent me a photo of her teaching her three year old son to make the chocolate cake. It is now her tradition to make this dessert with her son for his daddy's birthday.

"I think careful cooking is love, don't you?"

JULIA CHILD

Take time each day to really appreciate life, to soak it in. You can do that through a special dessert or a thoughtful text. Have you ever seen the red "You are Special" plate? My childhood friend, Judy, gave me that plate for my first birthday I was married. You set it at your table at the place for whoever is celebrating something. It comes with a permanent black marker, and you are supposed to sign and date it. I knew ours would fill up fast, so we never did that. You can revel in the goodness of life as you hold your sweetheart's hand or smile at a friend. Don't skip dessert. Master it!

Even though I can make a variety of desserts, whenever I ask my family what to make, they usually request that chocolate cake! It's fun to be known for something and to bless them again and again.

Savor every month

If you are married, you likely remember what it felt like to celebrate your first month of married life. Did you give your spouse a little gift or say, "Happy one-month anniversary"? Did you stop and celebrate that important milestone?

Scott and I were no different. As a young couple, we counted each month, stopping on the 21st of the month to savor our union of June 21. I chose June 21, which is the longest day of the year, because I never wanted our wedding day to end! (Well . . . not really! Our June wedding date just worked out that way!) We smiled a bit more that day and held hands more readily. We truly felt grateful for one another after one month, two months, five months, and ten months. It was just a chance to stop and thank God for another month together. The days were passing so quickly, and I loved acknowledging the passage of time as a couple.

While most couples stop counting months sometime during the second year, we somehow just kept up the tradition! We do not necessarily schedule a restaurant date or do anything special for every month we are married, but we do try to see who is the first to remember to say: "Happy anniversary!" We decided long ago that our monthly anniversaries would be our unique way to keep our marriage promises fresh.

I recall our 444-month anniversary. We decided to "do it up *big*!" We spent the night at Bay Hill Lodge, a local golf course designed and made famous by Arnold Palmer. The staff treated us to a dessert that read, "Happy 444-Month Anniversary!" They couldn't believe that after all our years, we still celebrate each other. For some reason, it always seems to make people smile when they hear that we acknowledge and celebrate each month.

Once we hit 500 months, we planned a special evening. We organized a getaway to savor this milestone. I feel so much gratitude for the privilege of being married to a wonderful man. Scott is one of my most treasured blessings. He is a wonderful husband, my best friend, a father, son, son-in-law, brother, brother-in-law, friend, business owner, board member, and so much more. There is no one on earth who I would rather spend time with. Why not let him know how I feel even more often?

As if counting months was not enough, one day Scott surprised me from a different angle. I received a phone call, and he told me, "Jennifer, we are going out tonight! It's our 1,000-week anniversary!" I thought, *Who thinks of these things?* I guess a former CPA!

Life goes by so quickly! I agree with Dr. Suess who wrote, "How did it get so late so soon?"

How did it get so late so soon?

DR. SEUSS

By now, you can tell I love celebrating big and small moments. It's usually not the big moments that make a great life as it is the small ones. People say, "it's the little things," and I truly believe it is. Bess Streeter Aldrich wrote, *It was true*, she thought, *that the big things awe us, but the little things touch us.*

I'm a big believer in the importance of holding hands; not many people seem to do it much anymore. I feel like it says to the world you are proud of each other, and you belong together. My parents, Vern and Bev Moline, have been holding hands for the 68 years of their marriage, and it always makes me smile to see them together. I love to hold hands with my husband, Scott. Scott is home to me. I could be anywhere with him on earth, and it would be home as long as we're together. I love him more now than I did when we married 42 years ago. In marriage, it's not the *big* moments that make it work, but a million little things that remind the other person how much they matter.

If you have never counted the weeks and months you have been married, give it a try! It's a fun way to celebrate, savor life, and connect to your loved one. People often tell me, "I have never thought to count weeks or months!" I just encourage them to jump in! Start now! It's okay if you haven't been counting all along. Start at any point, any week, any month, and see what you think. Something beautiful may be headed your way!

I'm a big believer in the importance of holding hands.

Enjoy afternoon tea

I'm a believer in tea. I really am. But, for me, it's not about the taste of the tea itself, but rather the moment, or should I say, moments? I just believe in taking a little time each day, or every few days, or even once a week to stop and slow down a bit. It does not need to take long. Ten to fifteen minutes will do just fine. It seems like we're always rushing from one thing to another. Now that I'm older, I've decided I'm done with rushing. I don't like it; I never have! It's hard for me to think straight when I'm rushing! I want to cherish time. I love this quote of an unknown origin, "Once she stopped rushing through life, she was amazed how much more life she had time for."

Teatime is a little interlude in the day and a quiet tradition I started a few years ago. I usually don't make any kind of a fuss. I simply heat the water, choose my tea, and find a quiet place in the house to have some self-guided permission to "sit a spell." Sitting down in the afternoon for a cup of tea might not appeal to you, but I am merely suggesting you take a few minutes to yourself, be it taking a walk or drinking a tall glass of water, and savoring a few deep breaths. I try to pay attention to the moment. Think of it as a little self-care and kindness for yourself. This is your reminder to slow down and breathe and see and feel every moment of your life.

Once she stopped rushing through life, she was amazed how much more life she had time for.

Often ascribed to C.S. Lewis, "You can never get a cup of tea large enough or a book long enough to suit me."

As you know by now, I love sending cards to people. It began as an occasional idea, but now I regularly try to tuck a tea bag and a pretty napkin inside the card. It's kind of become my "signature" without my intending it to be. Friends started telling me they hoped they would find a tea bag inside a card with a Jennifer Boyd return address on the envelope. It gives the makings for a cup of comfort. I love when friends text me a picture of their teatime.

Our little granddaughter, Margaret Frances, is just two years old, but I found an adorable red plastic teapot, cups, and saucers. The teapot is musical and plays the familiar child's song, "I'm a Little Teapot." She bobs her head back and forth listening to the music. I love to be with her. I can't wait for the day she and Gigi will have a real tea party together.

My reasoning behind doing this simple thing was to remind people that they are important and it's a good thing to take a little time for yourself. Slow down.

Share
the recipe

We treasure our moments on vacation, particularly in the mountains of Highlands, North Carolina. Gregory Wherry said, "Truly it may be said that the outside of a mountain is good for the inside of a man." The mountains refresh us. A good meal refreshes us, too. It became my tradition to prepare spaghetti sauce in advance. Spaghetti is "everyone friendly" with gluten free options galore; it's a go-to meal for me. I freeze it, and it travels well. Sometimes, it is part of our first meal in the mountains. But my spaghetti sauce recipe wasn't always so highly requested.

Years ago, I read of an older lady who was famous for her spaghetti sauce. Funny thing is, she would never share the recipe. After she passed away, people were sad, knowing they would never be able to enjoy her delicious spaghetti sauce again. Weeks later, as her children were going through her home to prepare it for sale, they discovered jars and jars and more jars of Welch's grape jam. Her secret was out! All those years, she was simply adding a tablespoon of the jam to her sauce.

After reading the article, I wanted to give it a try for myself. It wasn't long and my family started requesting my spaghetti for dinner, often boasting that their mom made the *best* spaghetti sauce! My secret? Whatever jar of spaghetti sauce happened to be on sale that week and a tablespoon of Welch's grape jam! That's it! I love sharing my recipes. To me, the greatest compliment you can receive is when someone asks for your recipe.

We loved when our kids would have a friend join us for dinner. I frequently got requests for "spaghetti and chocolate cake night" at our house. Two of our daughter's friends, Katie and Bethany, especially loved that dinner. Occasionally I would get a text asking if Mrs. Boyd would make spaghetti and chocolate cake for them. I loved those little girls, who are now mamas of their own children. I shared the secret with them, and they now make the famous spaghetti for their families. The joy continues!

As far as the chocolate cake goes, I'll share that one, too. It's not quite as easy as the jam in the sauce, but it's not difficult, either. If you love chocolate cake with homemade frosting, here's the recipe:

Fast Fudge Frosting

1 lb. box powdered sugar
1/2 c. cocoa
1/4 t. salt
1/3 c. boiling water
1 t. vanilla

1/3 c. butter, softened

Combine first three ingredients. Next, add boiling water, butter and blend with electric mixer. Next, add vanilla. Frost cooled cake. Delicious frosting and it really does taste like fudge! Enjoy!! love, Jennifer B

This recipe was given to me in 1980, the year we married. The giver's name was Mary Ellen, and although I have lost touch with her, I have never forgotten her recipe. I get requests for it often, and I hope you will, too. I use a Betty Crocker brand box cake mix. Having grown up in Minneapolis, I have a special affinity to the General Mills brand.

I have taught many of our friends how to make this cake, and it's always special to pass it along. Sharing a recipe or teaching a friend how to cook a family favorite spreads the joy to new generations!

Sharing a recipe or teaching a friend how to cook a family favorite spreads the joy to new generations!

Just be nice

Who do you see on a regular basis? If you stop and think about people you see every day, the first who come to mind might be your spouse, children, neighbors, or work colleagues. However, there are other people around you throughout the day. There are people who ring up the groceries or work in the post office. You might walk into the bank and interact with the teller. I always try to go through the check-out line that Ocnel, a new grandpa, is working at in our Publix. He exudes joy as he shares a picture of his first grandchild, Jamir. It just takes a few extra moments to be interested in people. Ocnel is from Haiti, and I just love his accent. We easily talk together as we walk to the car with groceries. He is the father of three daughters, so you can imagine his happiness to learn he has his first grandson!

One simple thing we can all do is . . . just be nice!

If I can, I like to visit with people who I run into throughout the day. There is a precious woman, Jasmine, at our post office, who has become a friend. I try to find her and go through her line when she is working. It doesn't take any extra time to make a connection, but it does take awareness and intentionality. We've never had any long conversations, but with a smile, there is warmth. Small gestures can mean so much to people.

Connecting with others begins with eye contact and a smile. Our little one-year-old grandson, Davis, can't talk much yet, but he sure can smile! "Your smile is your best accessory," said Allison Speer. Davis just loves to smile and wave! He can melt your heart. He has a new eight-week-old cousin named Palmer Houston who has just begun smiling, too. The smallest connection can be made with a little grin or a kind word. To make a big difference in someone's day, you might need a bit of bravery to start a conversation with a stranger, but I assure you that it's worth it. Give a compliment! If you notice something attractive in another person, just say it!

One simple thing we can all do is... just be nice!

People will say, "Thank you!" And your friendship can be off to a great start.

There is no need to wait for a big moment or a holiday. Opportunities are right in front of you constantly! Even when customer service representatives answer the phone, I ask, "How are you?" I have noticed that when you ask someone sincerely how they are doing, they appreciate it. It can be the beginning of a spark of happiness in the day.

1) What is your favorite dessert?

2) What desserts have you learned to make and which ones would you like to learn to make?

3) Do you have a favorite tea or coffee drink? Share it with the group.

4) Is there someone you connect with regularly in the course of your day that could use some encouragement?

CHAPTER TWELVE

The Heart of Simple Hospitality

Remember what is most important

When I was in my 20s, after graduating from college, I was considering going overseas to volunteer as a dental hygienist. I had wanted to use my skills as a hygienist in underserved countries. It had been a dream of mine for years. I got accepted to the program, and I traveled to Colorado for the summer for training. To be completely focused on the mission, I felt like I needed to end my relationship with Scott; it would be difficult to be in love with someone halfway across the world. We were dating, and I knew he was a wonderful man, but I wanted to be fully focused on whatever God was calling me to do.

Scott understood and was supportive throughout the entire process.

He wrote a letter that read, "I want you to go. I want you to do whatever God is calling you to do." He did not want me to live a life of regrets.

Along with the letter, he sent me a special gift. He knew I had a couple of small pieces of the blue and white Wedgewood china that I loved. He sent me a miniature Wedgewood vase. The man I loved mailed me a token of his love to keep. And I realized I may not see him for twelve months. In fact, I knew in my heart that I may not ever see him again.

Quite by accident, my roommate dropped the vase. It broke, and I was heartbroken. I watched it break into many pieces in what felt like slow motion. My heart was crushed along with it.

During the entire time I was in Colorado, I was praying about my future. Scott wanted to marry me, but he was so supportive and patient. He always encouraged me to follow my dreams and whatever God told me to do.

That summer taught me even more about his heart. I knew I loved him, and I knew I wanted to marry him.

The heart is far more important than the gift.

Even now, I have the little vase in our china cabinet. The glue still holds it together. I have kept it as a visible reminder about what really matters. Things don't matter. People matter. My roommate was more important than my Wedgewood vase. My love for Scott was the most important lesson in the story.

It's not about the thing. In fact, it's never about the thing. People are more important than things. The heart is far more important than the gift. Although we all like to give and receive gifts, the connection is truly what matters. A gift is just the vehicle to deliver love and thoughtfulness.

Your own version of hospitality

My version of hospitality has truly been one of the great joys of my life, but it may not be right for you. I invite you to use any of the ideas in this book to move you forward on a journey to a more beautiful life, but I also release you from the duty of it. If you feel guilt from one of these ideas, let that one go! If you feel delight, embrace that one.

Develop your own version of hospitality based on your unique personality, gifts, and situation. Just as there are unique fingerprints on every human, there are unique ways of loving others within all of us. Feel complete freedom to create rhythms in your life that make sense for you.

It's also critical to recognize your specific season in life, and move in accordance with the lifestyle that season needs. If you are in high school, your daily life is very different than that of a parent with young children. If you are a single adult or widowed, you may have more or less freedom to show hospitality to other people. If you have grandchildren or are approaching retirement, you may have more time than you ever had when your children were young.

You're not alive to survive... you are alive to make a difference.

You're not alive to survive . . . you are alive to make a difference. Do something with your life. Life is like a puzzle, and we all have a part; you have a part and I have a part. It's just a matter of figuring out what our part should be and then doing it. Do you know what your part is? I love the first line in Rick Warren's book, *The Purpose Driven Life*, where he says, "It's not about you." That's so very true. Let that sink in for a bit . . .

Don't let people go

People matter. Relationships make life rich! That is why I enjoy the mantra, "Never let people go." I think of my sweet friend Sara in Texas. She and I have not lived in the same town for thirty years, but we remain friends. We maintain a long-distance friendship by catching up on the phone periodically and sending texts when we think of one another. I cherish my long-distance friendships!

It doesn't take much time to text, send a card, or make a phone call. If a person comes to my mind, I just reach out! It's often very quick. If I drive by the place where a person works, I might say a prayer for him or her and send a text. While traveling, Scott and I might see a sign on the interstate that reminds us of someone, and we make a short phone call.

Recently, we were in Valdosta, Georgia, and we saw a barbecue restaurant that our friends, Beth and Blake, recommended. Even though we didn't go inside, we sent them a photo. When our daughter Anna was a little girl, one day she noticed the digital clock in the car said "12:34." Now, she's grown up and lives in another city, but when either of us notice that time on our phones, we stop what we're doing, and we text each other with an ever-changing emoji, just to let each other know we love each other and were thinking of one another.

Hospitality has two sides. One side is opening your heart, mind, and home to invite people into a relationship and invite them into the fun. The other side is holding onto people and letting them know they are worth the effort to remember.

Debbie, along with her husband, Chris, became our friends even as they were moving to another city. Debbie texted me a couple of days ago, and we are going to meet them in Atlanta. We have not seen them in eight years, but I know it will feel as though no time has passed.

There is just something about old friends. When someone knows you for many years, that person understands you in a special way that warms your heart. You don't have to explain yourself. Even when we don't see each other every day, we form a bond that can carry for many years. It may take some time to send a letter or reach out, but it is so worth it to hold on to a friend who has touched your heart.

Recently, I had one of the best days of my life. My precious friend, Lynn came over for a long-awaited lunch. We had become friends soon after my husband and I had moved to Florida as newlyweds. She was "a season ahead of me" in life, with children. I always loved and admired her as a mother. We lost touch, but I never, EVER forgot her. I would pray for her through the years whenever God would bring her to mind. I wrote her birthday of March 12th on my calendar every year for 28 years without knowing where she was celebrating. I had saved a birthday card I had mailed her back in 1993 that had been returned to me . . . just in case I were to ever see her again. What a thrill when I was finally able to give it to her in person! It seemed like no time had passed at all. That beautiful reconnection has been one of my greatest gifts.

Imperfect gifts welcome

Whether you are new to simple hospitality or a seasoned veteran, you quickly learn that every gift, party, or special event doesn't always go as planned. I give you permission today to move forward in your journey anyway. Some of my favorite moments in loving people well have grown out of imperfection.

Early in our marriage, we invited a couple to the house, and I had planned to create a blueberry lemon bar for dessert. I imagined it as a refreshing end to the evening with our new friends. As it cooked, I kept checking the oven.

Not done.

"I will just leave it in for five more minutes."

As I checked again, it still wasn't done.

"Okay, let it bake for five more minutes."

Some of my favorite moments in loving people well have grown out of imperfection.

This went on for a while, and I finally took the dessert out of the oven to allow it to cool. We spent time with our friends, telling stories during dinner and growing in friendship. When I served dessert, Scott tried to cut it, but that lemon bar was hard as a rock! He tried to salvage it by cutting harder, and he finally got a few "bricks" onto the plates.

Everyone sat quietly. They tried to cut it. They used knives and a little muscle until finally, one of the pieces went flying across the room! We all laughed until our stomachs hurt. In the end, it wasn't about the perfect dessert. It was about being together.

The meal, the card, and the gift are merely conduits to meaningful connection.

Now, many years later, the imperfection of that night is exactly what helps me to remember it. People don't remember every detail of the hospitality you extend, but they do fondly recall the joy of being in your presence. Hospitality is not just about offering a meal. It is ultimately about giving a piece of yourself to those you love or will grow to love.

I would call myself a catalyst for togetherness. The world is big, but I enjoy making it even smaller.

Share your hospitality ideas with me

Hospitality is a creative endeavor! It combines the fun of community with the high calling of making the world a better place, and I am always inspired by the way men and women serve others. If you have discovered a habit or a beautiful ritual that blesses others, I would love to hear from you. Share your inspiration and stories of simple hospitality that have blessed you and blessed the world.

Many of my favorite ideas have been borrowed from friends who tell me about the ways they enjoy serving others. This is a book of ideas, and I pray it encourages you. From the time I began dreaming about this book, I started thinking about you, the reader. I hope that this book provides a spark that moves you toward a more fulfilling and richer life. As you take chances and reach out to people, I pray for your courage! If you take a step of courage, tell me about it. You can send me an e-mail anytime at **simplehospitalitybook@gmail.com,** and I will do my best to respond.

I believe in the power of connection to infuse a lovely aroma of kindness into the air. Let's start a movement of people who hold the same intention. We intend to use each day to make the world a brighter place. It's not hard. It's a privilege! And I am always here to read about the joy you have experienced through your own journey.

I believe in the power of connection to infuse a lovely aroma of kindness into the air.

1) What stands out to you about this journey of hospitality?

2) What are some obstacles you would like to overcome to show more everyday kindness?

3) What ideas do you still want to implement for showing hospitality?

4) Do you agree that each person can make a difference in the world? How do you want to be remembered?

About
the author

Jennifer Boyd is living a life guided by a compass of faith and being thankful for all things.

Her greatest joy is her family . . . consisting of a husband, three children, two sons-in-law, and five perfect grandchildren. Her growing up family consisted of two wonderful parents and four younger siblings.

She has been married for forty-two fabulous years, yet she still feels like a newlywed.

She was given the gift of a happy childhood by loving parents.

She believes in slowing down and not missing moments.

She now relishes being Gigi to five precious little people.

She was named "Friendliest" in high school, and that trait has continued throughout life. Strangers are just friends she hasn't met yet.

She is always amazed at God's creation and is overwhelmed with His details in nature.

Young, married women and moms have always had a special place in her heart, and she has enjoyed mentoring and being mentored before it was even called that.

Most would say she has a pleasant and agreeable nature, some might even believe she owns a pair of rose-colored glasses.

Her dining room table is always, always, ALWAYS set . . . just in case!

She loves the sound of kicking the fall leaves, and since she lives in Florida . . . this generally requires a beloved trip to a chilly place with changing autumn leaves. She is so glad to live in a world where there are Octobers.

Conversation at the end of the workday is something she looks forward to with her husband.

Writing is something she must do. She cannot merely read her Bible, a book, or recipe . . . she must underline and write in the margins, as to never forget sweet memories.

She carries books and toys in the back of her car for grandchildren who request them regularly.

Her friends are precious to her, and she prioritizes staying in touch as best she can.

She has been known to hum because she's happy . . . and her husband has no idea what song it is!

She loves to hear the church bells and a train whistle in the distance.

She is grateful God made her just the way she is.

People often told her "You should write a book!" And now, after many years . . . she is taking their advice!

ACKNOWLEDGMENTS

Living life with gratitude and joy alongside people you love makes everything special and worthy of celebration!

Throughout this longtime dream of writing my first book, family and friends have walked alongside me, cheering me on with encouraging notes, phone calls, and faithful prayers.

My thank you could never be big enough nor my heart full enough to tell you how much I love you!

To my beloved husband, Scott, who never, ever gave up on me and believed in me when I didn't . . . you are the one who has made all my dreams come true!

To my wonderful children, Betsy, Michael, and Anna, and my son-in-laws Michael and Houston . . . Thank you for making life worthwhile.

To my precious grandchildren, Connor, Will, Margaret, Davis, and Palmer . . . you have filled my life with joy!

To my parents, Vern and Bev, who got me journaling as a little girl on our cross-country camping trips. I believe my love for writing began there.

To my one and only sister, Jeana, who we share mutual admiration for one another.
To my brothers Jim, John, and Joel, I have loved being your big sister.
To my "Southern Sister" Molly. We are sisters in our hearts.

To my BLC Sisters: Andrea, Ann, Anne, Betsy, JJ, Kristie, Sue, Susan, Tina, and Tracy . . . We are together forever!

To my long-time fourth grade friend, Judy . . . I treasure our friendship.

And now to thank even more friends who have made my life richer because you were in it . . . Beth, Brandee, Carrie, Cece, Darcy, Debbie, Hannah, Jan, Jill, Joanna, Lauri, Lisa, Lori, Lynn, Maggie, Megan, Miriam, Natalie, Sara, Shugie, Terri, Tracie, and Van.

This book would never have been written without the wonderful way Emily Osburne made beauty and order out of my scattered thoughts. What fun we had working together!

And to Mary Grace Burkett who captured my vision for what I wanted the book you are holding in your hands to look like . . . beautiful and inviting!

And to you the reader . . . you are my new friends!!

Gratefully,

Jennifer B

Made in the USA
Las Vegas, NV
02 August 2023

75560623R00136